Because of Katie

Dear Sweet Julie
God bless you

© 2011 KAREN BOREN GERSTENBERGER

Photo Credits:
front Cover photo of Karen & Katie Gerstenberger by Paul Dudley
Photography www.pauldudleyphotography.com.
Front Cover image design by Karen Gerstenberger.
Back Cover photo of Katie Gerstenberger by Philip J. Boren.
Photos on pages 155, 171 & 172 by Paul Dudley Photography.
Photo on page 196 by A.M. Ogle.

ISBN: 1466337346
ISBN 13: 9781466337343

Dedication

This was written because of Katie, our daughter Kathryn Emilie Gerstenberger, and all that she has taught us. She is a blessing forever. It is also dedicated to Gregg and David, the best possible traveling companions on this journey;

…to our family, as well as friends, neighbors and community, who sustained us with their daily love, caring, acts of kindness and generosity - for which we will always be grateful;

…to Bev Gaines and Maribeth Hinderer, for more than can be written here;

…to the staff at Seattle Children's Hospital, who provided a quality of care that was wonderful, beyond our dreams; to each nurse, doctor, specialist and staff member into whose care our daughter – and our family - was given;

…to Hospice of Kitsap County - especially Amy - with heartfelt thanks;

…to Heidi and Paul Dudley of Paul Dudley Photography, for your friendship, support and creative partnership;

…to Ellie & Phil Boren, for your support in every way (including supporting the publication of this book).

Special thanks to Ellie, Maribeth, Laura, Reba, Sara, Paula, Leslie, Anna, Georgann & Allegra - who read and commented on this book in its draft form.

I am grateful for the presence of Love during each step of this journey.

Table of Contents

The Story Before the Story

In May of 1991, Gregg Gerstenberger and I were married at the old Seabold church on Bainbridge Island, Washington. Seabold United Methodist Church held no religious significance for us, but was a treasured landmark on the way to my favorite place in the world: our family's cabin, built by my parents when they were newlyweds in the early 1950s.

Gregg's family had homesteaded a few miles farther down the road. We had strong, happy roots in this area, and we knew that we wanted to raise our children near our parents, in the healthy, saltwater-centered lifestyle that we had enjoyed as children: playing in the sand, wading, building rafts, rowing, fishing, roasting marshmallows over beach fires, digging for clams, crabbing, beachcombing for treasures and going to sleep with the sound of waves as a lullaby.

We built our home on the shore of Puget Sound, and Gregg commuted to the city for work. I worked part-time until it was possible for me to stop, and then I happily focused my energies full-time on our children, David and Katie, and our community. I was fortunate to have time to spend in classes and individual study, expanding and deepening my spiritual journey.

This hasn't happened without effort. I had graduated from college, got married and divorced, and held a variety of different jobs before meeting Gregg. Gregg had put himself through college by spending summers fishing in Alaska, and had worked in landscaping and as a ski-lift operator, before settling down to work for a large aerospace company.

Gregg enjoyed his job as a buyer, which allowed him to travel to faraway countries and immerse himself in their culture and language. We both love to travel, particularly in Europe. We love to walk and talk and eat well. I am a voracious reader and a spiritual seeker; Gregg is an agnostic, who enjoys reading - but often falls asleep when he sits down with a book. He is quiet, kind, intelligent, patient, strong-willed and loving (Norwegian/German). I am sparky, passionate, humorous, verbal, strong-willed and loving (French/German). Somehow, it works.

David was our first child, born in 1992. He was a quick learner who showed natural academic inclinations early in his life. He had a passion for cars as a toddler, which continues to this day, and a natural love of sports – tennis, golf, baseball, skiing and basketball. David skipped kindergarten and started the first grade in a "gifted" program in our school district, because he was doing addition, subtraction and multiplication *in preschool*. He was sweet, funny, kind and bright - an energetic boy with good self-management skills. He has always been a delight to us and everyone who knows him.

David embraced the arrival of his sister, Katie, in 1995 and has always been her closest companion and best friend. He never treated her as a rival; although they had their share of spats (just as all siblings do), he seemed to love her naturally, right from the beginning of her life. It is a blessing when your children choose one another as "favorite companion." David and Katie played together well and enjoyed a number of the same activities.

At the beginning of this story, Katie was a very social young girl. She loved her many friends, loved to read, sitting in her window seat, loved "Harry Potter" and "Pirates of the Caribbean" movies, and enjoyed watching television a bit more than we would have liked.

Katie was one of the few girls in her grade who was friendly with everyone. She was never involved in disagreements with school friends, but went along with the other girls to meet with a staff member for mediation, so that she would know what was going on! Katie was not a natural scholar, at this point; she was still a phonetic speller who preferred to socialize and focus on stories and dramatics. She was interested in pursuing acting and modeling, and had a natural emotional intelligence beyond her

Modeling portfolio photo, May, 2006

years. She could instinctively understand what was going on with the people around her.

Katie was a very pretty girl; even in elementary school, she received admiration because of her appearance. Her green eyes, dark hair and golden skin were a beautiful combination. She loved to look at herself in any available mirror, and enjoyed clothes (especially shoes), jewelry, shopping, and feminine treats such as manicures and elaborate hairdos. Yet she still loved to climb trees, play in the woods and on the beach.

Both Katie and David have innate athletic abilities. Attending swimming, golf and tennis lessons (and baseball camp) with David was not of particular interest to Katie, but they did this together over the years in the summertime.

We shared our love of music and theatre with David & Katie, taking them to live productions and concerts. They saw "Mamma Mia!" as well as "The Phantom of the Opera" on stage, and heard James Taylor live at the Gorge Amphitheater. They took piano lessons together and gave recitals.

Why Write a Book?

I wrote this book because I have been asked repeatedly to speak to groups about our experiences. It is my privilege to share what I have learned because of Katie, but it is not getting easier over the years – it's getting more difficult. In order to be able to continue to share this story with others, I decided to create a videotape; this book grew out of that project. It is written for everyone, laymen and medical professionals. Friends and family of patients, as well as patients themselves, will find resonance with the experiences told in this story.

The videotape and book are intended for use together or separately, as teaching tools, designed for medical students and professionals in all areas of that field. Primarily conceived as a seminar, the video covers the entire journey from before diagnosis through hospice care. It is broken into several segments, in order that it can be viewed a bit at a time and interrupted for discussion, or it can be viewed as a whole. *The intent is to encourage dialogue among peers and with mentors about how it feels to go through this kind of journey with a patient and her family.*

My deepest hope is that this dialogue will give medical personnel (and everyone who reads this book and/or watches the video) an opportunity to practice taking care of their own feelings about a health crisis, or about dying, so that they can in turn take the best possible care of patients, families or members of their community in times of crisis.

The death of a patient is traumatic to everyone who knows and cares for that patient and her family. It is imperative that each one of us learns how to take care of ourselves, so that we can transform our pain, rather than transmitting it to others. If this book and/or video help you to do that, then Katie and I will have had the privilege of giving you a real gift, straight from our hearts.

For information about speaking engagements, or to order a copy of the DVD, please contact me at karenlboren@yahoo.com . For more information about our life since Katie's journey, please visit my blog at www.karengberger.blogspot.com.

Thanksgiving 2005

CHAPTER 1:

"It's the End of the World As We Know It"

*I*n the autumn of 2006, I was deeply content in my life as a stay-at-home mother. For the past six years, I had been a volunteer in my children's schools and our community. I was excited to be embarking on an expanded role in a group I served, which provided "one-to-one Christian care to the bereaved, hospitalized, terminally ill, separated, divorced, unemployed, relocated, and others facing a crisis or life challenge."

Gregg was busy buying airplane parts from a manufacturer in Japan, a job which required him to travel overseas several times a year. David, a strong academic student, was a freshman in high school, on the tennis team for the first time. Katie had left the public school system and was in her first weeks at a private middle school – one that was specially attuned to artistically-inclined children. At the time, Katie's favorite subjects were reading and recess, and we hoped that attending a school which offered equal emphasis on the arts would help to strengthen her education.

Our family dynamic includes both sets of grandparents - who live about five miles away from us in either direction - with lots of aunts, uncles and cousins. We are a very close family. We did most things as a foursome - that's our way. Our children had a very secure upbringing, with lessons in tennis, golf, drama and swimming; vacations to Canada and California (where my parents have a home that we all enjoy). Generally, life centered on family, home, beach, school and church; it was a peaceful life.

During the first weeks of the school year, Katie began to exhibit a slight fever - and when that happens, you can't send your child to school, so I kept her at home. The fever would come and go, so she went back to school and then she'd have stay home – back and forth for a couple of weeks. I would drive to her school, pick up assignments and turn in what she had been able to complete. Then Katie started to be fatigued, and this was atypical – she's a very energetic person. This went on for three weeks. I took her to the doctor for blood tests; she had fecal tests, they tested her twice for mononucleosis - there were a number of tests taken - and everything came back "negative."

After three weeks of this - back and forth to school, back and forth to the doctor - I noticed a slight swelling in Katie's sternum. It looked like someone's thumb was pressing out, where there is normally an indentation. I pointed it out to Gregg, and he agreed that that wasn't normal for her, so we called our primary care doctor again. I had recently switched Katie's medical care from our (male) pediatrician to my own primary-care doctor, who had an excellent bedside manner, and was a good listener. She was a young, intelligent, well-respected, caring general practitioner (Dr. R.). She was also my mom's doctor, and since Katie was approaching puberty, I thought it would be more appropriate for her to have a female MD, and good for our doctor to have the full family medical history, spanning three generations.

Dr. R. asked me to bring Katie in for a scan - an ultrasound. Generally, when I had an ultrasound I would try to coax some information from the technician (I know that that's against protocol, but I think lots of people try to get information that way). This young lady was very professional and betrayed no emotions - and she wouldn't give me any information. She simply said, "The doctor will call you," just as they are supposed to say, so we went home.

Shortly afterward, I received a phone call from Dr. R. She told me, "We found something, and you need to get to the local hospital for a CAT scan *right away*, today." At that point, I couldn't breathe. She was talking and explaining the results of the ultrasound, and I said weakly, "You have to stop talking *now*." I remember sitting at the kitchen table, setting the telephone down and putting my head on my arms, - I had to work on catching my breath. Then I picked up the phone again, and the doctor said, "We found a mass in her abdomen; it looks like it's coming from the area of her kidney and heading towards her heart, so you need to get to the local hospital for a scan *today*." I hung up the phone and immediately called my husband, and told him, "They found something on Katie's scan; please get home as fast as you can - I don't know what's going on, but I have to take her to get a CT scan *now*."

Next, I called my mother, and asked her to come with me, and (bless her heart), she came right over. David stayed at home, while Katie, my mother and I got into the car and I drove to the hospital. Before we went in for the scan, my mom took Katie shopping at the hospital gift store, and bought a little stuffed dog for her. Katie was happy.

Katie had never experienced anything like this before, nor had I. She had to drink contrast dye, which tasted terrible; I was very nervous, trying to get her to cooperate and drink it all, so I was strict with her. She didn't know that anything was wrong, and I was trying to protect her from my concern, but also to get her to do what she needed to do - so we struggled through this, in the waiting room.

Katie was called back to the scan room. They allowed me stay with her, so I wore a lead apron during the procedure. She was very frightened, and I was, too but I was trying to be calm for her. She was put into the scanner and given an IV line. The medicine made her feel hot; it is frightening to a child to go through it, the first time. This heightened my anxiety, but she made it through the scan smoothly. Afterward, as a reward, we went to one of our favorite restaurants for dinner (Gregg was at home with David by this time). It's a family-oriented pub, with two floors. We were seated upstairs, and Katie ordered her favorite (the "Little Daddy Cheeseburger"), with fries and a soda. My mother and I looked at each other, thinking, *This is not good,* but Katie was oblivious to that. We finished our dinner and drove home. I never sit in that section of the restaurant anymore.

Our doctor telephoned again to say she had received the results of the CAT scan. Gregg and I were both on the telephone when she said, "There is a mass in Katie's abdomen; it starts on her kidney, and it looks as if it's just turning the corner toward her heart." She continued, "You need to go back to pick up those scans *first thing* in the morning, and catch the earliest ferry you can. Go directly to Children's Hospital through the Emergency Department. Don't check in – go straight to the ER. I have a (doctor) friend who is going to meet you there." That is how we first entered the hospital experience.

That was the first time that really bad news was delivered to us. It's important to stop and think about the effect of HOW it was delivered. This was a young doctor; possibly this was the first awful news she had to deliver to a patient or family. I had the impression that she was scared, and that terrified me.

> *That was the first time that really bad news was delivered to us.*

After the phone call from our doctor, Gregg and I put the children to bed, telling them what was planned for the next day, and then we went to bed. Both of us lay there, unable to sleep - I'll never forget that night. Gregg is a very calm, comforting person, yet I knew I could not turn to him for comfort, because he was just as hurt and frightened as I was. I remember cuddling up to him – with my back to his front, as we always do when we go to sleep - and feeling cold dread, knowing that there was nothing to do except wait until morning, and then take Katie and her scans to Seattle Children's Hospital.

On October 10, 2006 Gregg picked up Katie's scans early in the morning while I helped the children get ready for the day, and then Gregg returned to pick up Katie and me. We left to catch the ferry to Seattle, Katie bringing her favorite quilt in the car with her. David went to school and to tennis team practice afterward. We assumed that we would be back at home again in the afternoon, to pick David up from tennis practice. I was supposed to go to the dentist to have a broken tooth repaired, so I rescheduled that appointment as we drove through the city.

We went into the emergency department, and if you've ever been to the emergency department of the hospital, you'll know that the staff are very kind and calm, but let's be honest - it's not a place anyone wants to be with their child. They took us in as quickly as possible; our doctor's friend met us, as planned. We were put in a room, and they started an IV on Katie immediately, so that whatever they needed to do, she would be ready for it. They put a little splint on her arm - a little board to hold it steady - and she watched TV, to take her mind off of what was happening.

Meanwhile, several teams of doctors came into this private area of the emergency ward (we could shut the door and pull the curtains), and they asked us the same questions over and over again. The way I remember it, at least five teams came through, and we didn't know them - they would introduce themselves to us ("I'm Dr. So-and-So," and there were multiple student doctors with him), and they would ask us the same questions over and over again, about how this came to be: how it started, Katie's symptoms, her medical history, etc.

I thought, "We've already answered these questions; when is someone going to answer some of **our** questions?" I was upset because I felt that they were frightening Katie. They weren't doing this on purpose, but they appeared to be quite worried, and it was communicable. Since Katie had been healthy for most of her life up to that point, it was a strange situation for all of us.

> *I thought, "We've already answered these questions; when is someone going to answer our questions?"*

Gregg and I were invited to step out of the room briefly. We were told that, based upon what was visible in the scans, the growth pattern of the tumor looked like an adrenocortical carcinoma, but they weren't sure, and they wouldn't be certain until they could perform a biopsy. They said that Katie was *in great danger* - the tumor had entered her heart, it was friable and was growing throughout her abdomen – and because of that, she was going to be admitted to the hospital right away. There was no way that we could take her home, because the tumor was too widespread and dangerous.

We were stunned; we thought we were going to the hospital for more *tests*. I remember thinking in shock, "We don't have cancer in our family! This must be a mistake; we lead a clean, healthy life. This doesn't happen in our family."

In my mind it was as if a rapist had entered our house and attacked our daughter. She had been violated by a silent, unseen assailant. How DARE this tumor sneak in like that? Where were the signs? Where were the symptoms, when it was tiny enough to take care of it? Why not a peep, not a bump, not a bulge, not a blood marker, until it was encasing her adrenal gland, kidney, in a lobe of her liver, filling her inferior vena cava and in her heart? I was filled with rage, and terrified.

It is hard to adequately describe the quality of our fear. I could tell you about it in several ways, but the best way to set the scene is to tell you that, with the combined resources of the University of Washington Medical Center, the Fred Hutchinson Cancer Research Center, and Children's Hospital's own renowned doctors, we were told: "We never see this." "In 25 years, I have never seen this." "This is very rare in adults, and even more rare in children." "It is inoperable, and it is not chemo-responsive." Those words, spoken by deeply concerned staff, terrified us.

Gregg and I returned to Katie, taking turns going out of the ER to the parking lot to call our parents. I asked my parents to pick up David and spend the night with him, saying that Gregg and I were going to be spending the night at the hospital with Katie.

We were taken upstairs to a room on the cancer ward, with nothing but the clothes on our backs, and Katie's quilt. We were led into a double room with a family for whom English was a second language. We were as courteous as we could be, and as respectful of their privacy as possible. There was only a curtain dividing the two girls' spaces. Katie was in her hospital bed, and Gregg and I had an armchair that folded out into a single bed - and that's where we "slept," on our sides, huddled together that night. You can imagine that we didn't really sleep.

The sweet young girl who was in the bed behind the curtain was vomiting from the effects of her chemo, and walking to the bathroom, past Katie, Gregg and me with her IV pole in tow. She and her mother were speaking Spanish to one another, and we felt as if we'd landed on another planet or at least, another country.

The next couple of days are a blur, frankly. During one of the first nights, I walked out of Katie's hospital room, and talked to one of the night nurses, just outside the bedroom door. I felt quite disoriented, yet this nurse was so compassionate, so calm and understanding, that she gave me confidence. I could tell that I wasn't the first person she'd met in that situation. I wasn't all alone in no-man's-land; I was with friendly, kind-hearted, caring, capable people who wanted to help my daughter and me to cope in this new world. This was powerfully encouraging.

We were shown around the ward and learned about different areas of the hospital. An important place to know: the linen closet, where we could get extra blankets, towels and hospital pajamas for ourselves and Katie (until we could get home to retrieve our own). Because Gregg and I had only the clothes on our backs - we had not even a toothbrush - we were given all of the "overnight" things that we needed. We learned where the parent showers were (several floors above the cancer ward), where the snack rooms were, the laundry room, lounge with computers and printers, resource library, gift shops, as well as the cafeteria and the coffee shops; where all the parent bathrooms were (because there are only two bathrooms for parents on the cancer ward, sometimes, one has to leave the ward - and sometimes, leave the floor, even in the middle of the night - to be able to freshen up or take care of your needs). We started to understand the hospital's resources and routine.

Meeting our Childlife and Social Workers for the first time, I thought, "Why do we need a Social Worker? We don't beat our children," only to find out how much one *does* need a social worker in the hospital world. We needed Childlife daily! The two who worked most closely with us, Julie and Tanya, made such an effective team that their respective areas of expertise blended seamlessly. We were introduced to a nutritionist, physical therapists, chaplains, psychologists, palliative care (now called "advanced care") and other technicians across many disciplines. There was even a financial advisor to help us to navigate the hospital-billing process. We needed nearly all of them, and people often appeared *before* we knew we needed their assistance. These specialists are essential in cancer patients' and families' lives.

At first, it was a bit overwhelming, meeting so many people across disciplines that were new to us; it took some time to become accustomed to having our quiet, ordinary, private life invaded. Over time, we felt grateful that our needs were understood, anticipated and met by the staff at Seattle Children's Hospital.

> *At first, it was overwhelming, meeting so many people across disciplines that were new to us; it took time to become accustomed to having our quiet, ordinary, private life invaded.*

Julie from Childlife visited Katie regularly. In the beginning, she brought presents – a brilliant way to begin. We had several excellent Childlife workers, but Julie bonded particularly well with both David and Katie. She introduced us to the Caringbridge website (www.caringbridge.org), which was great tool for us. It's free to hospital patients, and was a great way for us to stay connected with our family and friends. I met some wonderful people on caringbridge, and found it to be an enormous support. In fact, I think it must have been much harder to deal with a cancer diagnosis before the age of the internet. We were able to be connected and supported, without being exhausted.

Unfortunately, when something like a child's cancer diagnosis occurs in a small community, rumors start to circulate; I received phone calls and messages from people saying, "I heard *this* or *that*," and I didn't have the time or energy to correct rumors. I told people, "If you see it on caringbridge, you can believe it, and if you don't see it on caringbridge, don't; if you want to know what's going on, refer to the caringbridge site." That was helpful to us in saving time and emotional energy.

On the 13th, Katie had her biopsy, and from that, we received the initial diagnosis. Having the biopsy was terrifying for her, because she had a great fear of any kind of surgery. In fact, one of the first things she said when we got to the ER was, "I'm not having surgery!" We said, "We're just going to see what happens, and find out whatever you need to help you."

A biopsy is a small surgery, and we had to agree to it in order to get a clear diagnosis. Katie was taken down to the surgery department, and we went with her. A surgical Childlife worker helped to explain the procedure to all of us. Katie was given some medication to help her relax, and I was allowed to go with her into the operating room.

Waiting on the gurney where Katie was going to have her procedure was a

> *Waiting on the gurney was a Beanie Baby, and seeing that relaxed her - and me. It was a sign that we were in a children's hospital - a place where they understand the heart of a child."*

Beanie Baby (a little stuffed red bird), and seeing that relaxed her - and me. It was one of the special signs that we were in a *children's* hospital - a place where they understand the heart of a child. Katie got up on the gurney, and I leaned over to kiss her. I was sitting on a stool which had wheels under it; when I leaned over to kiss Katie, the stool tipped over, and I started to fall. All of the staff converged on me, as if I was the patient - it was embarrassing, because I didn't want to create any "mom-drama," but it made us laugh. I must have looked as if I was fainting, but I wasn't – the wheels on the stool simply slid out from under it. That was an awkward, funny moment in the midst of a tense situation. Katie was relaxed and drowsy by the time I left the operating room.

David took the day off from school to be with us and support his sister. We went to the cafeteria, and then back to the cancer ward to wait for Katie. When she was wheeled into her room on a gurney, she was "higher than a kite," and saying funny things. As the drugs started to wear off, we told her some of the things she had said, and she thought that was hilarious; she asked us to tell her over and over again. I think that drug was called Versed; the staff called it "happy juice."

After the pathologists had an opportunity to re-view her biopsy, Gregg & I were taken into a private room with the attending physician, Dr. Matthews, and told that the pathology was not conclusive, but that it looked most like a neuroblastoma, judging from its growth pattern. She said that a Wilms' tumor was an-other kind of tumor that involved the kidney (and was easier to cure), but Katie's didn't look like a Wilms'.

Dr. Matthews told us news that was very hard to bear: the tumor had started on her left adrenal gland and encased it and her left kidney, then crossed the midline to enter her liver, and had grown upwards and completely filled her inferior vena cava, ending in her heart. Because it was "friable" or flaky, Katie was in danger all the time - a piece of this could break off and enter her heart or her lungs, and she would die instantly. The surgeons had been consulted as soon as we got to the hospital, and they refused to perform surgery on Katie because they said she would certainly die on the operating table if they tried to remove this enormous, unstable tumor.

The surgeons said, in effect, *We don't operate on people who we know are going to die. She needs to have chemotherapy first and see if you can solidify this tumor, and shrink it, and then we will reevaluate whether or not she's a candidate for surgery. Right now we cannot - your only choice is to try chemotherapy.* The tumor was so large that it was assumed to be Stage 4 (though Gregg and I didn't use that term).

We cried a bit, and then we asked the Dr. Matthews, "Is there a treatment plan for this?" She answered, "Yes." I said, "I'm so glad to hear that. I was starting to really *dislike you*, because all you ever did was give us bad news. But it now sounds like you have something we can do for her." We then asked her, "Will you tell Katie for us? We can't tell her this,"

> *I said, "I'm so glad to hear that. I was starting to really dislike you, because all you ever did was give us bad news!"*

and to our relief, the doctor said, "Of course I will; that's part of my job. Your job is to comfort her."

All three of us went into Katie's room and sat with her. Dr. Matthews told Katie that the tumor was cancer, and that she thought it was neuroblastoma. She said, "We're going to start your chemotherapy right away. To have it, you will need to move to the intensive care unit, so that you can be monitored a little more closely, and you will have a private room."

Katie never warmed up to Dr. Matthews after that, though she is a perfectly nice and highly-skilled oncologist. Katie simply never forgave her for delivering such devastating, life-altering news; I imagine that is a terrible part of the job of an oncologist. I will always be thankful to Dr. Matthews for shouldering that burden, and thus allowing us to be Katie's comforters.

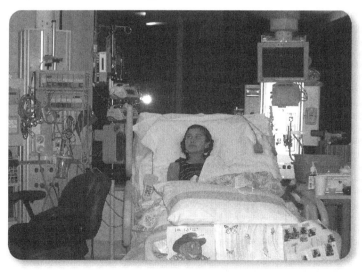

In the ICU to begin chemotherapy, October, 2006

I remember going outside of the ward to use a telephone in a quiet area. I called my family and told them of the diagnosis – that the doctors thought the tumor was a neuroblastoma - and laughing crazily, saying, "When you're celebrating because you think your child has a neuroblastoma, you know that life has taken a really bad turn, because *no one* celebrates a neuroblastoma diagnosis!"

Our only happiness in the diagnosis was learning that there was a protocol available, and that Katie could begin treatment right away. It was one of those gallows-humor, sarcastic moments when you feel like doing a cheerleader jump and saying, *"HEY! We got neuroblastoma!"*

Katie was moved to the intensive care unit, and was hooked up to monitors via little sticky dots and wires - monitoring her heart rate, blood pressure, oxygen levels, etc. They used state-of-the-art machines – equipment was all around a big, sterile room. We were trying to make the best of it, so my husband asked Katie, "How do you like this?" indicating the private room with big windows. She looked around and said, calmly, "It's a little high-tech for my taste," and then settled in to watch the TV. As soon as we could get them from home, we used family pictures and posters from teen magazines to decorate Katie's room and make it less high-tech and institutional-looking.

Katie had no roommate in the ICU, but all of the patients in the ward are obviously very sick, so it was more restrictive than the cancer ward, which – hard as this may be to believe, has its fun/crazy side. On the cancer ward, there are tricycles, wagons, computer games, and more people walking around, talking, eating, visiting. We had to keep quiet, and had to leave the ward when we needed to eat or use the toilet.

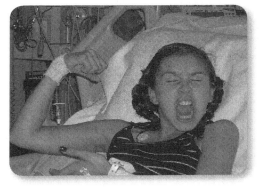

"Gun Show" in ICU, October 2006

The patients in ICU are constantly observed, visually and/or with monitors, one nurse for each patient, so privacy was non-existent. Katie was one of the only children in the ward who was conscious, and it gradually became clear to us that the nurses enjoyed taking care of her, because she was a delightful, spirited, fun girl – and she was awake.

The hospital has some wonderful provisions for patients and families – some are simple, yet comforting. One example of this is the warming ovens provided for blankets. Whenever a patient feels chilly, it's easy to get a warm blanket from the oven. Occasionally, people forget to replace what they take out, or the nurses are too busy to refill them, so after learning where the linens were kept, I would refill the "oven" when I took one out for Katie. The snack rooms for patients and families on all the wards are stocked with popsicles, graham crackers, saltines, soda and tea. Each one has a refrigerator/freezer where you can store your own favorite foods. These little touches are important to making the hospital a "home away from home," especially if you are living there with your patient for weeks – or months.

One important thing to note about patients and families in the hospital setting is the fact that, no matter who we are in the "outside world," we are stripped down to our essence in the hospital world. Whatever our job, our title, our level of education, income, our home environment, our socioeconomic milieu, our looks, our self-image, our background – none of that is of any value or importance in a health crisis. We are only exactly who we are at the moment the crisis occurs, nothing more or less.

Wealth, advanced degrees - even religious beliefs – nothing is of any consequence except who we really are, inside. What we **think** or what we **believe** will crack very quickly under the stress of our child's illness; our essence, our deepest truth, arises out of the ashes of our former life. The families you meet will be stripped down to their essence. They might try to flex and show you some of their more impressive qualities, but cancer is a great equalizer.

There are no shortcuts or advantages in the cancer

> *No matter who we are in the "outside world," we are stripped down to our essence in the hospital... it is good to be mindful that the people you encounter are, to a large extent, more naked than they have ever been, and more frightened.*

ward. We are who we are, and – as with old age – in the stressful environment that is a pediatric cancer ward, we become even more who we really are. So it is good to be mindful that the people you encounter are, to a large extent, more naked than they have ever been, and more frightened. They are facing life and death issues, some for the first time ever, and they are finding out that they cannot take anything extraneous with them on this journey. My experience confirmed for me, that *leading with love* is the only way to make it through the hospital journey.

In the first days of Katie's admission to the hospital, I could not eat. You can see evidence of it in our photos; I don't know how much I weighed when we went into the hospital, but I know I lost some pounds right away, because I couldn't eat anything but tea and crackers - I was literally sick to my stomach about everything that was happening to Katie. The chorus from "It's the End of the World As We Know It," by R.E.M. kept running through my mind.

At this time, Gregg went home every night to be with David, seeing him off to school in the morning, and then coming to the hospital to be with Katie and me during the day. This was uncomfortable for us, because

> *We asked Katie, "What can we do to give you the most support? What would help you the most?" She answered, "I want us to be together as much as possible."*

we were accustomed to living close together at home, so we asked Katie, "What can we do to give you the most support? What would help you the most?" She answered, "I want us to be together as much as possible." So Gregg informed his employer, and was told that he could put all travel on hold; he was able to cut back his work day from 8 to 6 hours – basically, whatever we needed, they supported - in addition to providing a fantastic health-insurance plan.

As soon as Katie's diagnosis was given, David voluntarily withdrew from his school at home, moved to Seattle with us and enrolled in The Hutch School (which the Fred Hutchinson Cancer Research Center has created with the Seattle Public Schools). It is a private school within the public-school system, for patients, siblings and children of patients, who are being treated at the Seattle Cancer Care Alliance (also known as SCCA; it comprises the University of Washington, Fred Hutchinson Cancer Research Center and Seattle Children's Hospital).

To illustrate how perfect this school is, no students can attend the Hutch School when they are sick, so there is no risk of infection for any family member – a huge issue for cancer patients.

The school day is from 9:00 A.M. to 1:00 P.M., and it's tailored to the needs of a child with a family member who has cancer. Whether the student is the patient, or a relative, the school is adapted to support each child who has been thrust into this strange situation. Many students attending the Hutch School have had to move away from home - some from the other side of the country. Some live in a hotel; some live at Ronald McDonald House. It is a real melting-pot - the one similarity between the kids is the fact that someone in their immediate family has cancer. There is a therapist on staff who meets with the students regularly; there are fun activities and exciting field trips. The program is well-balanced, and simply stated, it is a gift.

All of these changes made it clear that we needed to change our residential situation - commuting was too hard on Gregg and David, and their absences were hard on Katie and me. A friend of ours had lived at Ronald McDonald House during her son's treatment for a brain tumor, so we knew that was an option. We looked into it, with help from the staff at the hospital, and made an application. We were quickly assigned a room at Ronald McDonald House, which is just a couple of blocks away from Children's Hospital.

Gregg slept in our room at the House Sunday through Thursday nights with David, while I slept in the hospital with Katie. On Friday and Saturday nights, Gregg moved into the hospital with Katie, and I went to Ronald McDonald House with David. In this way, each child had one-on-one time with each parent. After five consecutive nights of sleeping in the hospital, I desperately needed to sleep in a more private place so that I could catch up on rest. Ronald McDonald House is a wonderful provision for families under the intense stress of a child's illness.

One of us was always with Katie in the hospital. I love the fact that Seattle Children's Hospital does not

I love the fact that Seattle Children's Hospital understands that we know our child better than anyone.

restrict "visiting hours" for parents and caregivers; you are always welcome to be with your child, even during tests and procedures. The hospital actually welcomes parents to sleep in the patients' room; they provide a cot, and bedding for it. We eventually brought our own things to make ourselves more comfortable, but we were always made to feel welcome and part of the Katie's essential team.

The staff understands that *we know our child better than anyone*, and that our presence with our child is the greatest comfort to her. They often said that they were the authority on medicine, and we were the experts on our family – an attitude that was comforting, respectful and empowering. We became a team, working with the staff for Katie's best health care interests.

After Gregg and David settled into our room at Ronald McDonald House, David came to meet me at the hospital each morning, so that we could eat breakfast together; then he took the shuttle from the hospital to the Hutch School with other students. When he returned from school each day, he spent time with Katie and me. There was very little homework, because they perfectly understood the stress these kids were enduring. Because David had been in a "gifted" program at home, I wondered what was going to happen to his education; I need not have worried. He had special tutoring a couple of days a week, so that he could keep up with his program, and he made great strides in science. He had a science tutor who is a researcher at the Hutch Center - one-on-one science instruction! He also had one-on-one math instruction, and he finished the school year exactly where he needed to be, in order to move up to the next grade. Kudos to the Hutch School!

The hospital had its own school program for patients, with a teacher who held classes in a schoolroom in the hospital, or would meet with patients individually in their rooms, if they were too sick to go to the classroom. The hospital staff helped us with all of the information and paperwork so that Katie could move her schooling to their in–house program. Though it became impossible for her (Katie quickly became too ill to study), she did start the program. My feeling was that she needed some constructive activity, needed to keep her mind busy and growing, and needed to believe in - invest in - her future. Watching TV and movies, and even reading, was not enough to focus her mind forward, but school came to be too much for her, once her chemo regimen was established.

Sleeping in the hospital is not restful; I was always desperately tired, and learned that I had to wear earplugs at night in order to be able to sleep. The nurses went in and out at all hours to take temperature, blood pressure, hang medications, etc. Sharing a room with another family multiplied the interruptions. I told Katie, "If you want me, and I don't hear you, throw a stuffed animal at me" (she had received an assortment of stuffed animals as gifts). Early one morning, I was awakened by a thump on the head from a stuffed dog which Katie had thrown; a lab technician had arrived to take a blood sample, and Katie wanted me to hold her hand. Permission to throw something at Mom was a small effort to bring humor (and control) into Katie's daily life.

The ICU was the ward in which I really started to grasp how to live in the hospital. One of the first doctors we met there, Dr. Brogan, is a treasure - and will be, in my heart, for the rest of my life - because of the way he interacted with all of us. Not only did he take excellent care of Katie, but he bonded with David, as well; their friendship goes on to this day. This doctor made all the difference to me.

When Katie was first admitted to the hospital, we learned how a typical day is structured; in the ICU, rounds took place between 7:00 and 7:30 in the morning. I developed a routine of getting up by 6:30 A.M. and going to take a shower. I would go up to the fifth floor, take a quick shower and put on basic makeup, because I always wanted Katie to see that I "had it together." I never wanted her to think, "My mom is really losing it; she doesn't even care how she looks anymore - so I must be really sick." I kept it simple: eye shadow, mascara, lip gloss, gel for my hair, and that was all. I would be dressed and ready for rounds, just as if I was attending a business meeting; in fact, that is what rounds are: the business of your child's health care.

In the ICU, with one nurse to each patient, you know that your patient is as safe as possible, because there is always a pair of highly-skilled eyes trained on the monitors (or on your child). Initially, I felt mystified by the environment, and didn't understand how to interact with the staff or how to help Katie. I was raised as a Christian Scientist, and, though I had left that church some years before, I was still relatively ignorant of the medical world. I had never spent any length of time in a hospital, except when recovering from childbirth or surgery – certainly not as a *caregiver*.

Living with the awareness that, at any moment, Katie's life could end, I surreptitiously watched her like a hawk. I was especially afraid, whenever I had to leave her, that while I was away, she might die. Consequently, I didn't like to go to eat; it was stressful every time I had to use the bathroom or take a shower. I was always in a state of heightened alert. I had a pager, so when I had to leave - even to use the toilet - I could be paged, but it was terribly stressful to leave her side.

At rounds one morning, Dr. Brogan was surrounded by student doctors, Katie's nurse and me, and they were discussing Katie's case. Dr. Brogan looked at me with great compassion, and asked, "Are you getting out at all?" I replied, "We've been told that she could die at any minute. I don't want the moment of her death to arrive, for her to look around for her mom, and I'm at *Starbucks*!" Dr. Brogan took a breath - a moment's pause. Then he spoke to me with great tenderness, and said, "I think you can get coffee; you can take a walk and get some fresh air. I think she is stable enough for you to safely do that."

> *I will always remember that moment, because Dr. Brogan didn't minimize my fear.*

I will always remember that moment, because he didn't minimize my fear - there was a very good reason for fear in those circumstances. However, the way that Dr. Brogan dealt with me showed that he had *heard* me. By taking a moment of silence, he showed thoughtfulness, listening and respect, after which he said something useful and helpful to me, with which I could work. So I started to take a brief walk every day; I ate meals and was able to use the restroom without being completely stressed. I became a little bit calmer.

Because Gregg was at work six hours a day, and David was at school, they do not share many of my memories of events which occurred in the hospital - some of which impacted me deeply. One pivotal experience was caused by Katie's heart rate. It was irregular, because the tumor had entered her heart. One day, I was standing in the ICU, just outside her room, which had a sliding glass door. Suddenly, a lot of people hurried into Katie's room - very quietly, but swiftly - and they took a cart with them. I had a sort of mother's intuition about what they were doing but I didn't know for sure, because no one had said anything to me.

The Fellow on duty at the time was the team leader, and many staff members gathered in Katie's room watching the monitors and awaiting his directions. The Fellow was watching the monitors silently - very intently - and I was watching him, Katie, and the staff in her room.

They stuck paper paddles on Katie's chest, under her T-shirt, and stood waiting for him to give an order, and I remember him saying, "Everybody, just stop." In my memory of it, there was complete silence and stillness - and then he said, "I think she's fine," and they all quietly left Katie's room. I understood afterward that they thought they were going to need to shock her heart. It beat in a strange rhythm due to the tumor's location.

To watch that happen to my child, especially without warning, was a traumatic event, and it is one of the moments I'll never forget: watching a group of people rush that cart into her room, while I stood by - helplessly, dimly suspecting what was going on - but not believing it. And watching them file quietly out of her room, while my insides collapsed.

> *To watch that happen to my child, especially without warning, was a traumatic event that I will never forget.*

While Katie was in the ICU, she learned that she qualified for a wish from the "Make-A-Wish" foundation. She was so happy about this that she cried happy tears, and told my mother excitedly about it. My mother knew that it meant that Katie was very ill indeed, but she showed only pleasure and excitement to Katie.

The Make-A-Wish representatives were kind and generous. They came and got acquainted with Katie, brought gifts to her, and put time and effort into trying to grant her wish. She asked to be in a Harry Potter movie; when she was told "that's not possible," she wanted to be an extra in a TV show. Not possible. She thought about a shopping spree in New York, with a stay at the Plaza Hotel, but we told her that we could arrange that for her – she needed to think of something that we couldn't give her. She wanted to meet Miley Cyrus. Not possible. She worked on her ideas for months, but unfortunately, none of them came to fruition, because she dreamed so big!

Katie weathered the first round of chemo very well in the ICU. The oncology nurses had to come up to the ICU to hang the chemotherapy drugs, because they are specially trained for that. Childlife, a chaplain and our Social Worker visited us in ICU, which was comforting.

We had one of the greatest nurses of all time in ICU, and she bonded very closely with Katie and David. She brought in nail polish, and she painted Katie's toenails and fingernails and washed her hair in bed, and tried to help her feel clean and feminine again. Katie did start to be sick from the chemo in the ICU, so we knew she needed anti-nausea medications, and that began a whole new world of medical education for us. After she finished her 1st round of chemo and was stable, the doctors said, "We think she's well enough to move back down to the cancer ward and to have her chemo there," so we were moved to the SCCA ward.

CHAPTER 2:

On the Cancer Ward

Gregg and I soon realized that we had to adjust the way we dealt with David and Katie regarding TV, movies, and computer time while we were in the hospital. We felt that our children needed to have as healthy an upbringing as possible; he and I were both beach-loving children, so we had gathered our resources and found a piece of property with woods and beach access. We built our home so that our children grew up playing in the woods, on a rope swing, on the beach and in the water. We limited their television and computer time to one hour a day on weekdays, and 2 or 3 hours on weekends. We favored Public Broadcasting shows, and introduced the children to Masterpiece Theatre and mysteries. Once Katie was admitted to the hospital, and was not allowed to move around because the doctors were afraid that a fragment of her tumor could break off at any moment and kill her, her activities were severely restricted. David's activities changed, too, because his life revolved around the Hutch School, Ronald McDonald House and the hospital.

For the first time in Katie's life, she had unlimited access to television and movies, and she was happy about that; she spent a great deal of time watching TV. Meanwhile, I was twiddling my thumbs, feeling frustrated and concerned about what was going on in her mind, the fact she was getting behind in school, and was consuming the kind of TV programs that I would normally prohibit. Childlife supported us in our attempt to keep our family rules and dynamics as "normal" as possible, but you have to flex somewhat when you move from home into a hospital setting. We looked for classic movies, such as ones that were made in the 1950s and 60s, which were fun for all of us to watch. Katie did some reading, but not as much as I would have liked her to do.

Since Katie was going to receive 5 rounds of chemotherapy, she needed a central line through which the team could administer the medications without constantly sticking her with needles. Because of the location and wide-spreading of her tumor, Katie was not candidate for either a port (subcutaneous port-a-cath) or a Hickman line (a type of intravenous catheter). Initially, she had peripheral IV lines placed in her feet and her arms, but soon the staff told us that their plan was to give her a PICC line. When they explained it to us, it terrified me, because they said that they were going to thread very tiny tubing through a blood vessel in her arm and pull it almost all the way into her heart, to allow the best access for medication. I was in favor of the quickest and best access, but was terrified that they were going to puncture her heart, a blood vessel or disturb the tumor and kill her. I didn't trust the procedure - I didn't trust the whole concept - yet it was a commonly-used technology, and it was the best on offer. It had to be done.

When the team was on the way to her room to perform this procedure, Katie was given medication to help her feel relaxed. Katie was always funny, but when given those drugs, she was even funnier than usual. The team came in, and (though I grew to love this technician later), when I first saw the woman who was going to perform this delicate procedure on my daughter's body, I could not believe it. She looked more like somebody who would be on the entertainment staff - she was very freewheeling, a little blasé, and not super well-groomed, in my perception. I remember that her hair was dyed - it had grown out noticeably at the roots, and they needed a touch-up. I felt, if you're casual or careless like that with your appearance, how can I trust you to get this PICC line in the right place for my child's health and safety?

Though I know it had nothing to do with her skills, I was terrified to allow her to put anything in my child's arm and wire it *into her heart*, because her appearance wasn't tidy enough to give me confidence in her precision with the instruments. It was one of those moments when we had to act on faith in the hospital. We had to trust that this person was a highly skilled, experienced and trained professional - the hospital trusted her; she had performed this procedure successfully hundreds of times for other patients.

> *Right or wrong as it may be, appearances can create unexpected responses to the team.*

So we sat there nervously, while this sort of free-wheeling-looking person quickly and competently put a double-lumen PICC line in, and did it without pain or complications for Katie - all was well. As I said, I grew quite fond of this woman, as I became more familiar with her. Right or wrong as it may be to make superficial judgments, appearances can create unexpected responses to the team.

After Katie completed her first round of chemotherapy, I felt that she deserved a wonderful present. I had a ring which my parents gave to me when I graduated from high school, and I was planning to give this ring to Katie when she graduated from high school. However, given the uncertainty of the circumstances and what she had just been through, I thought it was an appropriate gift for this rite of passage. I gave her my eternity band of small diamonds and emeralds, and told her "I was planning to give this to you when you are older, but you're mature enough now for the responsibility – you've just been through a very mature experience."

After that, she always wore the ring with pleasure and pride. We did our best to celebrate the end of each round of chemo; we brought in a fabulous, custom cake from a local baker for the end of Round #2. We celebrated because we wanted Katie to feel our admiration for her accomplishments, as well as to mark the passing of difficult milestones - and to remind Katie that she was actually getting past those milestones, and closer to the end of treatment.

Early on, we were paid a visit by a member of the palliative care team, and I didn't understand why they would be seeking us out in the beginning of Katie's treatment. I assumed that palliative care meant, "We're out of treatment options; she's going to die;" that was my interpretation of what it meant. Now, I know better; I know that palliative care is comfort care, and that it can be necessary in a "life-limiting situation" as much as in an end-of-life situation, but at the time, it frightened me to see someone from that team in Katie's room, so I became angry. The palliative care representative was not a bad person, but I took an immediate dislike to him, associated him with an abusive person from my past, and never got over it. I knew that this was in part an emotional reaction, but something was triggered in me that I couldn't erase.

Although I listened to what he had to say, once he left the room, I told our Childlife specialist and Social Worker, "I don't ever want to see that man in here again. If we need palliative care, we will call for them." Occasionally, we would run into him around the hospital, and I would smile politely and say as little as possible.

I suspect that most human beings have "background programs" which are operating all of the time, and in such a stressful situation, we can experience an intense reaction to someone that has little or nothing to do with him as a person. In addition, the impulse to "shoot the messenger" can arise due to a bad reaction to the message. You may encounter some of this with patients and their family members, because we are all individuals with unique histories – and you may not have the opportunity to know us well enough to understand what is behind these reactions.

> *In such a stressful time, we can focus an intense dislike on someone that has nothing to do with him as a person.*

Checking email in the cancer ward, October 2006

We were learning about Katie's susceptibility to germs and about the immune system. We used hand sanitizer everywhere - whenever we walked into and out of a room. There were signs everywhere "Gel in – gel out." We were given the gift of scented hand sanitizer, and that was nice to have on the bedside table, in a purse or a pocket. Some of the scents bring me back to the cancer ward – I avoid those fragrances now - but they are a good present to give to someone in treatment for cancer.

After we moved down to the SCCA ward from the intensive care unit, Katie's hair began to fall out. Katie had long hair, which she had grown out since she was young; it was very important to her. It's possible that she believed she would be one of those people who did not lose their hair - I have read that some cancer patients believe this - but it started to come out in strands, a bit at a time, and then, in clumps. It was itchy, so she would scratch her head, and then look in her hand, and to her dismay, there would be a bunch of her hair. I brushed her hair to ease the itching, and tried to get the hair out of the brush and into the waste basket without her seeing it.

One day, seeing how much of her hair was in the wastebasket, she burst into tears. I sent Gregg and David right out of her room - this was a matter for the women. I held Katie in my arms while she cried and grieved over the loss of her beautiful, long hair. She was only 11 years old, and even though we know that hair grows back, to a child, it takes a long time!

We talked about what steps we could take to make this less painful for her. There are several kinds of wigs: real hair, synthetic hair, partial wigs which you wear with a hat, and the option to shave your head and embrace baldness. Katie wanted a human hair wig (which is more expensive than synthetic, but also more natural-looking), so we decided upon that purchase, as well as a synthetic one that she wore with a hat. This made her feel a little bit better able to deal with the loss of her hair. When they arrived, however, Katie found that the wigs bothered her – they made her head itch - so she wore bandannas most the time. There were a few hats which she liked, but mostly she wore a variety of colored bandannas, leaving little strands of her remaining hair sticking out the back. Even with these accessories, the loss of her hair was a great blow to Katie.

Typically, it takes about 3 weeks to recover from a round of chemotherapy, for your blood counts to come back up and to get strong enough to endure the next round of treatment. In between, patients have daily injections to boost their immune system, and those shots HURT. They were necessary each day, until her blood counts rose and she was no longer neutropenic. The drug prescribed for Katie was called GCSF, and it cost about $1,000 per injection. We were so thankful for our medical insurance! The nurses gave Katie her shots in her thighs or arms (trading off to give each area a rest), while Gregg and I helped to numb the area beforehand with ice packs or numbing cream. We also provided comfort by allowing Katie to squeeze our hands, or holding her in our arms during the injection.

Blood clots (or bits of tumor – the doctors weren't sure which) had been discovered in Katie's lungs, so she had to have two additional shots every day, morning and evening, of a drug called Lovenox (a blood thinner). The nurses were very kind, patient, cheerful and compassionate when preparing and administering these injections.

Katie endured blood draws, blood pressure and temperature checks in addition to scans and injections, and she tried to block out as much of this as possible by reading and watching movies and television. I wanted her to study her school books, and to try to attend school in the hospital, but unfortunately, that became impossible as the rounds of chemo progressed, because she experienced increasing nausea and weakness. When she started the cancer treatment regimen, the staff did not offer her every kind of medication to mitigate the side effects; they waited to see how her body reacted, and then offered medications appropriate to the effects she was experiencing.

Amazing as it may be, our children had each vomited only twice in their lives; we were not used to dealing with vomit, and I regret to have to admit that Gregg and I were both squeamish about it. It took us a little while to learn how Katie was responding to the medications, to anticipate the nausea, and for Katie to understand what was going on in her body. As we learned these things through her experience, we also learned about the medications available, which ones worked best for Katie, and how to ask for what we needed. Even the anti-nausea medications had their drawbacks; for example, one of them caused Katie to experience leg tremors, so that one had to be discarded. It was a steep learning curve.

The Infectious Disease team (a group – a bit overwhelming) stopped by to see Katie, because she had developed a rash - a side effect of one of the medications – and they asked a series of questions, to help them discern whether this was a new disease, or a reaction to a drug. They were very polite, but it was surreal – first, discovering that Katie had a very advanced tumor, and then answering these questions which did not seem to apply to Katie's case. Since the Hematology-Oncology team had seen a similar rash in other patients who had been treated with this same drug, I thought the questions were a bit silly, but we answered them straightforwardly. It is, after all, a teaching hospital!

After we had a diagnosis and treatment plan, we put the word out to all of our friends and family about it. We have some friends who work in the field of cancer and immune system research, so we sent out e-mails and phone calls, and asked everyone who had any knowledge of any kind, or any connection that they could use anywhere, to find out as much as they could about this disease and to send us all the resources they had. We needed to know who were the experts in the field, whether we were in the right place, if we needed to move to some other hospital, if there was anything that we were missing – anything and everything that we could think to ask, we did. As we received replies, I made notes, and eventually, I had a piece of paper filled with input from cancer researchers and people "in the know." I was holding onto that list, in order to ask questions of the next attending physician (they change every few weeks). The next attending physician to take care of Katie, Dr. Park, had been described to us as the expert on neuroblastoma, and I was very much looking forward to meeting her.

When Katie found out that she had cancer, she decided that she didn't want to hear about the medical details. She gave us a clear message: "I don't want to hear about it; if you're going to talk about my cancer, leave the room." That was not my preferred way of doing things; I would have preferred to include Katie as much as possible in all discussions so that she felt empowered and a part of things. However, Katie was like her father in many ways, and drew upon her Norwegian heritage when she chose her way of dealing with her illness; she was quiet and stoic about a great deal of what she endured. She seemed to "put her head down" and concentrate her energy on simply getting through it; she didn't verbalize her feelings about her illness very often, and she didn't want to hear us talking about it, either.

Children's Hospital is very family-centered and patient-centered, and the patient is always included and informed; children are not treated as lesser human beings, and the staff does not talk over a patient's head. So Katie was always initially included in discussions, but when she had heard enough, she would ask us to take the discussion outside, and we respected her requests. A consequence of this was that I didn't talk on the phone very much from her hospital room; I maintained contact with the outside world chiefly through e-mail and the Caringbridge website.

When Dr. Park came on service, she met Katie and our family, and eventually, we took our discussion into the hall, outside of Katie's room. Dr. Park is not much taller than I am, so I looked her in the eye, and said, "I have this piece of paper, and this is my due diligence; I need to ask you some questions. We've put the word out to everyone we know, and these are the suggestions and the names that they've given me. I need to know what you think about these suggestions." I went through the list of researchers and facilities - names of doctors and experts in the field - and one by one, Dr. Park replied: "I know him; I work with her...my husband works with her; this one doesn't apply. This is not that kind of cancer; they don't do that; we have that here," etc. We went down the list, item by item, and she showed me that she already possessed all of the information which I had unearthed to offer her.

> *It was imperative to me to communicate to this doctor who & what kind of family she was dealing with; I needed to know that she had the same level of commitment that I had, & I needed to see it in her eyes.*

Then I looked straight at this doctor, and said, "I need to know that you will not let money or logistics stop you from getting my daughter the help she needs. If you need money, I will get it; if you need an airplane, I will get one; if we need to move, we will move. I need to know that *you will stop at nothing* to get Katie whatever she needs to be saved from this."

Dr. Park looked seriously at me, and said, "I never would let any of those things stop me." That is when I knew that we could work well together - that I could trust her completely. Meanwhile, my husband was standing nearby, practically collapsing from embarrassment, but I had to have that conversation with Katie's oncologist; that was my job as the mother of my daughter. I needed to know that the team would leave no stone unturned in searching for a cure.

Ask any mother whose child's life is threatened – she will stop at nothing to save her child. It was imperative to me to communicate to this doctor who and what kind of family she was dealing with; I needed to know that she had the same level of commitment that I had, and I needed to see it in her eyes. She showed me that she was trustworthy, knowledgeable and committed - and so we began our working relationship on a strong footing.

The staff felt that, even though her life was still very much in danger, Katie could safely take a bath. We developed a routine around bath times, because the few tubs are shared among many patients, so you have to be organized and respectful of your allotted time. I would sign up for a tub room at a certain hour, in between Katie's infusions of medicine. The nurse would unhook her IV and put protective parafilm around the lumens and protective wrap around Katie's PICC line. I would run the water very warm, with scented bubble bath in it, get extra towels and flannel blankets, as well as fresh, clean clothes, and set it all up in the bath room.

I helped Katie walk down the hall, undress, and get into the tub, where I would wash her hair, give her a scalp massage, and we would talk. She loved to talk in the bathtub, and she liked me to read to her. Katie relaxed and enjoyed the floating sensation and the warmth of the water. She was given cute flannel pajamas and matching t-shirts which were very stylish by an aunt and uncle, and some luxurious underwear from Juicy Couture by another aunt and uncle. As I helped her dry off and get dressed after her bath, I hoped that these items of "tween" style would help her to feel as good as possible. I would then gently brush what was left of Katie's hair, tie her bandanna in place, put the wet towels and linens in the hamper, and gather up her dirty clothes to take back to Katie's room.

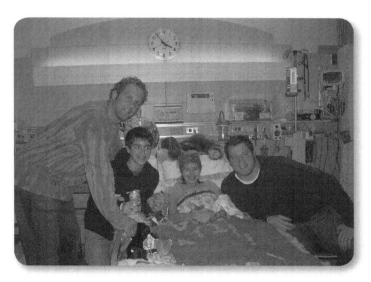

A visit from two of the NFL's Seahawks, 2006

At this point, Katie was able to have very gentle physical therapy. I worried about her losing ground physically, losing her natural fitness. Picture an active girl, who had been hiking 6 - 8 miles in the summer, swinging on a rope swing, happily yelling, running up and down stairs, performing in drama camp - and now she was bedridden, with a gigantic, yet invisible, tumor in her abdomen. What Katie really wanted was massage - she was carrying stress in her body. Gregg and I would give her massages practically every day, at her request. The physical therapist, Linda, also gave Katie massage, worked with her on range of motion, and did what was considered safe for her condition.

This physical therapist won my heart by "thinking outside of the box:" she helped Katie create a gift for David's birthday. Linda is also a chef, and her family owned a bakery when she was growing up. She asked Katie, "What does your brother like to eat?" Katie replied that he liked lemon bars, so Linda gathered the ingredients, brought a pan

> *Katie's physical therapist won my heart by "thinking outside of the box"*

and helped Katie to make those for David. Linda then took the pan of batter, baked the bars, and brought it all back so that Katie could give this to David for his birthday.

Since she wasn't allowed to leave the hospital, Katie couldn't get to the store to buy anything for her brother; because of the creative thinking and compassion of this wonderful physical therapist, Katie was able to surprise her brother with a handmade gift which he truly loved. This activity got Katie out of bed, standing up, stirring, and doing something for someone else. That was part of her physical therapy at Children's Hospital – a combination of occupational, physical and emotional therapy. That is excellent family-centered care.

A nutritionist worked with Katie, and this was vitally important, because she lost her appetite – another side effect of chemotherapy – she not only lost the pleasure of her sense of taste, but she was nauseated by the smell of food. Losing her appetite led to losing weight – and Katie was already slender. One of the most helpful things was the fact that the wonderful hospital kitchen allowed Katie to order and eat whatever she desired. For days on end she ate Cocoa Puffs! After some time, she couldn't look at another Cocoa Puff, so she began to order from the kitchen – things like fresh strawberries (even in winter), Oreo smoothies - whatever she could eat, they would prepare for her. That was a happy surprise of family-centered care.

It was hard, in the beginning, to see Katie order food and then not eat it; as a parent, I felt bad about that, just as you would in a restaurant, or as a guest in someone's home. This is an area where the rules are different, in the hospital. Katie did her best, but chemo killed her appetite. She lost so much weight that you can see the change in the pictures. She simply couldn't eat enough to keep up with her body's need for calories. The decision was made by the team that she had to have a naso-gastric (NG) tube placed, and this was a very traumatic experience (for both of us).

Picture this: I sat on the exam-room table with my legs apart, with Katie sitting between them. I held her in my arms, and our Childlife worker told us what was going to happen, and suggested some tricks that Katie could use to make the placement easier. The NG tube is a long, thin tube with a weight on the end. A nurse pushes it through the child's nostril, down her throat and into her stomach. The child has to swallow it, and try to keep from throwing up while it's being forced down her throat. As a mom, I was there for comfort, so I simply held Katie in my arms while the nurse quickly and deftly shoved the tube down her throat. Katie gagged and was miserable. She didn't want the NG tube in the first place, and it was a very difficult experience, but the tube was placed on the first try. Katie was lucky, because her tube stayed in place; a lot of children vomit so hard that the tubes come out. Toddlers are known to pull them out, and some of their parents even learn to replace them!

After having the NG tube placed, the feeds (which are liquid food, hung in a plastic bag on the IV pole and run over several hours through the NG tube) were Katie's main source of nutrition. It was best to run them at night, so she could be freer of encumbrances during the day. She was unable to swallow pills, so we put some of her medications through the NG tube, either by crushing them and mixing them with a liquid, or requesting that they be dispensed in liquid form. That was one of the benefits, for Katie, of having an NG tube.

Nasogastric tubes can develop clogs, and we learned to deal with that issue with the help of the nurses, who taught us that soda pop can be used to dissolve clogs. One night, toward the end of Katie's last chemo cycle, her NG tube clogged, and it was preventing the nurse from administering her feeds. Katie was asleep when the tube developed the blockage; her nurse began to talk about pulling out the tube and replacing it.

I thought, *"You are **not** going to take that thing out and make Katie go through re-placement."* The nurses are used to this - it happens frequently – they are busy, and after a few tries, if the clog doesn't budge, they naturally think, *This tube has got to go.* But the placement was a traumatic experience for Katie, and I didn't want her to have to go through it again. I asked the nurse, "What can I do to help? I don't want her to have to get a new tube." The nurse said, "Try pushing soda pop into her tube, and see if that will dissolve the clog."

I got a can of soda from the snack room, drew some of it up into a plastic syringe, and pushed it gently into Katie's NG tube, but the clog wouldn't budge. I tried every kind of soda pop they had, pumping it in and trying to draw back on the NG tube to dislodge (or dissolve) the clog. I did this on and off, all night long, trying not to awaken Katie, until the clog finally gave way.

Katie didn't have to have another NG tube placed; I felt like "Rocky" – I could practically hear the music from the triumphant movie scene playing in my head, because I had saved my daughter this one bit of distress and hassle. On the cancer ward, there is so little we can do to protect our children, but that was one of the things that I could do, and it gave me great satisfaction.

Katie had Tegaderm stuck on her cheek to hold the NG tube in place, and when it wasn't in use, she could wrap the tubing with a rubber band and clip it to her clothes. She got so used to it that she often didn't bother to secure it, but let it hang down. Sometimes, people would stare at her, particularly after she lost most of her hair and had the NG tube stuck to her cheek. That bothered her, which was interesting, because Katie stared at other people (though I tried to teach her not to do so). She still stared at people when she was having treatment for cancer, but it annoyed her when others did it to her.

The doctors prescribed many different kinds of tests and scans during Katie's treatment. Some of the tests were more stressful than others. Katie had ultrasounds, echocardiograms, CT scans, PET scans, X-rays and MRI. MRI can be unpleasant because it's very loud and claustrophobic. The patient lies down in a tube, and once the scan begins, the tube emits sounds as if it is being beaten with a huge hammer. Katie was allowed to wear headphones in the MRI, thank goodness. Gregg and I were in the room with her to add comfort, and we were able to wear earplugs

One of the early tests was an MIBG scan. It used radioactive dye, in the hope that the tumor would take up the dye and show itself clearly on the MIBG scan, providing helpful information to the team. It was a long day, during which Katie was not allowed to eat anything, while I worried about her discomfort and the delays. After many hours, we were finally taken down to the scan. Gregg and I sat with Katie while she lay still on the table. The MIBG scan didn't work, in this case – Katie's tumor did not take up the dye - so she endured a very difficult day for nothing. This search for information is one of the things that one has to endure during treatment for a rare disease.

When a doctor ordered a scan, we complied, but doctors need to know that some of these are very stressful to the child and therefore, stressful for parents. When a child is suffering and there is nothing you can do to mitigate that suffering, it's very hard on her family. To watch your child suffer, when you want only to protect her, and take her pain away – to endure that, over a period of days, weeks and months, is hard work. Even the nicest, best-mannered, kindest person will show strain under such conditions. Put us into a melting pot with other families who we've never met before, in a place where none of us wants to be, with a life-threatening illness in our precious child's body, and you have a recipe for interesting (sometimes complicated and intense) interactions.

> *To watch your child suffer, when you want only to protect her, over a period of days, weeks and months, is hard work. Even the nicest, kindest, best-mannered person will show strain under such conditions.*

By this time, some of our closest friends and family had come to visit, and that cheered us, but it was easy to see that it deeply disturbed some of them. Some people are better suited to dealing with the hospital environment than others. Some of our family adapted beautifully and were perfectly natural, comfortable, and great company when they visited; some people behaved as if they were at a funeral, and it was an emotional weight when they came to visit. At a certain point, I asked a relative, "Please tell the others not to come, if they don't like being here. I can't comfort them; I need to take care of Katie, and if they can't take care of themselves, they should stay home. We appreciate the effort, but it's not helping us." So a number of people didn't come back, and that was fine; I got to be pretty free and frank about stating the truth.

Some people showed up without asking first, and that was usually a mistake. My best friend is a cancer survivor, and she knew exactly what to do; she would say, "I do not need to see you; I'm going to sit outside in the lobby and knit, and if you want me, I will come in. I'm perfectly capable of entertaining myself." She was great, easy company no matter what was happening, so she was always welcome.

Because my grandmother had been a board member of the hospital for 25 years, we received kind visits from some of the staff. Nana Emilie loved Seattle Children's Hospital with a deep devotion - it was one of the greatest loves of all of her charity work. The president of the hospital came to visit us, as well as a board member. This was very kind of them, to take time from their busy schedules to seek out a family they had no need to meet. Unfortunately, I was out - getting a bite to eat or in the restroom - when they visited. Both of them left a message, and I remember saying to my husband, "I know I should be impressed by these kind visits from important people, but all I really want to know is if they have a cure for Katie's cancer."

It was a moment when I realized that I had become extremely focused. Life becomes very simple in the cancer ward, and if a person is relevant and helpful, they are most welcome. If they are not central to what you are doing, it is difficult to find the energy to pursue the connection. There were times when other parents of patients wanted to get acquainted, but I simply didn't have the energy to reach out and bond with new people.

After we spent a few weeks in the hospital, it was time for Halloween. Patients cannot go trick-or-treating, but the staff tried to make the holiday as much fun as possible. Katie wanted to dress up as Elizabeth Swann (from the "Pirates of the Caribbean" movies), and she wanted a top-quality dress. Because we had our hands full at the time, we felt it would be acceptable to get a costume online, so one was ordered. When it arrived, I was pleased; it was a very nice costume. While she was polite about it, we could tell that Katie was disappointed, because the quality of the dress wasn't as high as she had hoped it would be. I loaned her a pair of my most beautiful slingback pumps (brought from home - they matched the dress), and that helped to satisfy her. She wore a sort of pirate hat to cover her hair loss. Overall, the costume wasn't quite what Katie was looking for. We made the best effort we could, but spending October 31st in the hospital does not really feel like a Halloween holiday to a child.

On the cancer ward, there is a bathroom in each patient room - for the patients only. It is forbidden for parents to use the patient bathrooms, and that rule makes perfect sense, because if a parent is in the bathroom at the time when a patient needs to use it, that creates a problem. Patients rightly have priority. Every patient receives a bin with his name on it, which is placed on the toilet (it looks like an upside-down hat, and it is called a hat). Patients are asked to urinate in the hat, so that the nurses can measure their fluid output. After each patient uses the toilet, he is supposed to remove the hat from the toilet, place it on the floor, and call the nurse, who will measure the contents, and then dispose of it.

At the time when Katie was a patient, there were only two parent bathrooms, and perhaps 25 (or more) patient rooms. You can do the math, and see that there were a lot of us using those two toilets. The parent showers were on another floor. In the middle of the night, if you had to use the toilet, you had to leave your child's room - and if you were modest at all, you needed some coverage.

I didn't own any suitable pajamas, so I called a personal shopper at one of the local department stores. I said, "I am coming in - I have very little time. Please can you find some pajamas that are modest and warm? I also need a pair of comfortable shoes, as I will be on my feet all day." I had noticed that the nurses (who were on their feet all day, too) wore either light-weight rubber clogs or heavy-duty ones, so I requested a pair of clogs. A sweet young lady had it all ready for me in a dressing room when I arrived. I tried everything on, bought what I needed, and was on my way back to the hospital in record time. I would recommend this approach to anyone.

Because it is so difficult to sleep in the hospital, when you have to use the toilet in the middle of the night, you want to go as quickly as possible, and get right back to bed. If the toilets on the ward were in use, I had to leave the ward and go down the hallway to find an empty bathroom; at times it was necessary to go to another floor, depending upon how crowded things were in the cancer ward.

One night, as I left the ward to go to the bathroom, I encountered the mother of another patient in the hall. English was her second language, so she spoke with a heavy accent, and I tried to understand her through my drowsiness. She told me that she had quit her job (a food-service business, delivering sandwiches to workplaces) in order to be with her daughter in the hospital. Her home was on the other side of the state; her husband was there with their other children. One of those children had contacted her and said, "I need new shoes, and we don't have any money."

That was the night when it dawned on me that it could always be worse.

It turned out that her husband was gambling and had lost their money. He was the only remaining source of income for the family - the one in charge of the other children - and he was gambling their money away. I did my best to comfort this sweet lady, and then I went to the bathroom.

Returning to bed, I continued to think about her and her difficulties. That was the night when it dawned on me that it could always be worse. The next day, I told my husband, "It could be worse - I didn't think it could get worse, but it could! At least we have family nearby, we are solvent financially, and we are all here together." I found out, over and over again during the next months, that things could have been much worse than they were for us, even though we felt we were in the worst possible situation – living every parent's most terrifying nightmare. It was an awful awareness, but it opened my heart; I realized that I could not feel sorry for myself, because someone right next door might have all of the same problems we had, *and more.* Some families have terrible troubles in addition to pediatric cancer.

My husband and I married and started our family in our 30s, so we were older than many of the parents of our children's friends. We worked diligently to be responsible, to save for our children's college education and our retirement. We enjoyed a modest lifestyle but an interesting and happy one, and we put family at the center of it. We worked at staying fit and providing healthy food; we taught our children about their heritage - they were learning French, and living in a Norwegian town - they were exposed to the dramatic arts and music. We took the children on fun vacations and outings, spent time together in nature, were involved in their schools and activities; in short, we gave them the best upbringing we could.

All of our efforts to be good parents did not keep our daughter from getting a rare form of cancer. On top of that, to find ourselves in a situation with people who didn't even have the skills and tools that we had was a mind-expanding and heart-expanding experience. To go from a secure and loving home life, which we had intentionally built - working, saving, teaching and supporting each other, in order to make a happy family for our children – and to be thrown into the depths of the human experience, has changed us profoundly.

At the time when we embarked on this path with Katie, I was engaged in my own spiritual journey. I was accustomed to awakening before my children each morning to spend quiet time in prayer and devotional reading. That private, peaceful luxury came to an abrupt end, just when I needed it most! However, one of the blessings of having devoted time to my own spiritual path was the fact that, when I needed to draw upon what I had studied, I found it was within me. I learned which devotional was the best for me (*Radical Grace* by Richard Rohr); I could just take in about one page each day, and then live it, as best I could. Spiritually, this taught me a great deal about the difference between belief and knowing.

I found a quote which sums up what I felt at this time - it is from Dietrich Bonhoeffer, a German theologian who died in a concentration camp in 1945:

"There remains for us only the very narrow way, often extremely difficult to find, of living every day as though it were our last, and yet living in faith and responsibility as though there were to be a great future."

CHAPTER 3:

Chemotherapy and Outpatient Life

*D*uring rounds, or when specialists (such as the Infectious Disease group) came to see Katie, one senior doctor and a group of residents and/or students would appear in her room. There might be as many as eight people in the room at a time. Having her privacy violated in this way made it difficult, at times, to welcome these visits. Often, we felt like saying, "I'll talk to *you* (the doctor in charge), but the rest of the crowd, please step outside." To the great credit of the staff, they supported us 100% in asking for what we wanted, and respected Katie's wishes; no one ever acted as if they took offense. This was not a personal rebuff, but it did wear on Katie to be a subject of teaching; I imagine she may have felt a bit like an animal at the zoo.

In November, Katie had her second round of chemotherapy. She had another biopsy, with pathology using an electron microscope, because there was not a conclusive answer from the first biopsy as to what kind of tumor this was. Unfortunately, the second biopsy was also inconclusive, but the attending physician felt that it was it was adrenocortical carcinoma, which is even more rare than neuroblastoma. This required a different treatment protocol, so Dr. Park contacted the one hospital in the country which studies this particular cancer: St. Jude's. Dr. Park works closely with oncologists all over the country in the Children's Oncology Group – they share research – so the doctors at St. Jude's provided the protocol for Katie's new chemotherapy regimen, in order to address adrenocortical carcinoma.

I began to feel concerned, because Katie was becoming depressed after a couple rounds of chemo, and understandably so - the life she knew had been wrecked. Even though we were giving her as much support as we could, and gifts, cards and messages of encouragement were flooding in from all over, Katie had lost the life that she loved. She was still alive, but she had lost *her* life, the one she should have been living - that of a sixth-grader, going to school, seeing her friends, with age-appropriate concerns and activities.

I asked for a consultation with someone on the psychiatric team; I wanted someone to come and evaluate Katie, to see if there were something we could offer her, such as therapy, or other options. I knew that the staff would have seen depression in the cancer ward before. The chaplains were a wonderful support to me, but Katie wasn't as interested in spiritual resources as I was, so those didn't help her a great deal. After I requested help from the psych department, three people arrived.

Imagine Katie, sitting up in her hospital bed, with three strangers sitting around her in their chairs. I was standing behind the psych team; Katie looked at me over their heads, as if to say, "Why did you do this to me? What am I supposed to say to them?" She put up with the invasive, intrusive questions - which were intended to help diagnose her problem, but were clearly making matters worse, at that moment. The team left after interviewing her, and, to be honest, I don't remember any outcome from their visit. Perhaps they established a baseline impression of Katie's mental state, but her depression continued unrelieved, for the time being.

By the time that Katie was under the care of her fourth attending physician (in the rotation), the team decided that we should all be allowed to move to Ronald McDonald House. I said to the kind doctor who broke the news of Katie's impending move to outpatient care, "Why are you sending us out now? Everyone has said she's in danger; she has a friable tumor, and we were told she couldn't move." He replied that she was doing well up to this point, and that she was stable. They felt that she would be happier, and would have a better quality of life, outside of the hospital than in it. Perhaps that was an outcome of the psychology team's visit.

This move sounds like a great thing, but I want to stress here how frightening it was for us. Moving out of the hospital into Ronald McDonald house meant that we were going to be solely responsible for Katie's medical care – away from doctors and nurses - giving her all of her medications and her shots, monitoring everything that happened day and night, and making decisions.

Because I had been raised as a Christian Scientist, I did not go to a doctor or take medicine until I left that religion, when I was in my 30s. At this point, in my mid-40s, I still wasn't too knowledgeable about illness or medication; I could give my children their over-the-counter pain medication or antibiotics for ear infections, but shots? Not me! I felt that Katie was so sick that we should hire a nurse to help us – she deserved *professional* care. I argued with the hospital staff about this, and they replied (very kindly and respectfully, but in effect), "We've taught less intelligent people than you, and we *will* teach you. We teach everyone!"

When I first heard this, I felt offended - I thought we were being strong-armed, and felt that we should have other options - but what they knew (and we didn't, at that time) was that our daughter would prefer our bumbling efforts to an expert's care. She did not want another stranger introduced into her life. We went so far as to interview a nurse through a home health care agency, but Katie vetoed her right away…so Gregg and I were drafted into the pediatric nursing corps.

We learned about all of Katie's medications, the doses and scheduling, and we were taught to maintain Katie's PICC line, and how to flush it twice a day with heparin. We learned how to prepare her feeds, operate and maintain her feed pump. In addition to her twice-daily shots of Lovenox, there was a third shot each day (GCSF) after each round of chemo, which helped to boost Katie's immune system. Because of its high cost, the medication was kept in a locked refrigerator at Ronald McDonald House. It had to be kept cold, and it was a viscous liquid; though she was brave and had grown accustomed to the Lovenox, the GCSF injections hurt Katie, every time.

Gregg (who has actually passed out at his own blood draw) and I were both given instruction in how to give injections. We practiced on a "dummy" arm, and a nurse invited us to practice on her arm. I did not like that idea at all, but we did practice, became less squeamish, and eventually, we developed basic skills for giving injections. Gregg is the one who ended up giving her shots; the first time I tried to do it, Katie flinched, and I pulled back on the needle – I couldn't complete the injection. This is an illustration of what a wonderful man Gregg is: he overcame his great aversion to needles, and he gave her all of her shots smoothly and efficiently. I kept the schedule, drew up the medications, cleansed the area where the shot would be given, held her hands for comfort, gave her baths, maintained her PICC line, dispensed all of her other medications, but I wasn't good with needles.

Katie with Gregg in our room at Ronald McDonald House, November 2006

The four of us moved into the room we were assigned at Ronald McDonald House. We were happy to finally be all together in one place, even in a small room. There was an armoire with a TV and DVD player, a table and two chairs, two queen-sized beds and a window-seat bed. We had our own bathroom, with a tub and toilet; this was a great luxury to us, after hospital living. A sink, mirrors and cupboard were next to the bathroom. We were allotted a couple of cupboards and a mini-refrigerator in the kitchen, oriented to the lobby, pantry, laundry room, playrooms and computer area.

Most of our meals were eaten at Ronald McDonald House with many other families, and our family was assigned a chore each week to help maintain the House. I slept much better at Ronald McDonald House than in the hospital, though ear plugs were still sometimes necessary.

We spent a portion of November in Ronald McDonald House, celebrating Thanksgiving there with extended family. Each year, a volunteer group comes in and prepares a real Thanksgiving dinner, with turkey, stuffing, potatoes and all the trimmings - everything you could ever hope for - not institutional style - delicious! They did a fabulous job, and generously sacrificed spending Thanksgiving at home with their own families in order to serve ours. Katie was not hungry and didn't want to participate, but at least we were all together, and enjoyed the meal as best we could.

That was a particularly difficult holiday for our children, because we normally spend Thanksgiving week in California with my parents, at their winter home; it is also the week of my mom's birthday, and David's birthday, and our family tradition is to gather in the desert for that special week. We had to cancel our plans, and the children were terribly disappointed.

When we found out that Katie was very sick, my parents asked how they could help us, and I surprised myself by making this request, "Please don't go to the desert; please stay here with us - we need you here." They unselfishly stayed in Washington for most of the winter, giving up their warm-weather activities and "snowbird" social life, and were a great support to us.

Katie's first outpatient "day pass" (a permission slip from the doctors to take a patient out of the hospital and Ronald McDonald House) came at this time. We got in our car and drove to a pretty shopping village near the hospital so that Katie could walk around and do a little bit of shopping. I was afraid that she might catch a virus of some kind, since her immune system had been attacked by the chemotherapy, but it went well. Though Katie was relatively passive about the experience, we felt that it was good to get her out of the cancer-care atmosphere, even for a short time, and it was good for us, as well.

The doctors' idea had been a good one: living at Ronald McDonald House did indeed improve some aspects of our situation. Katie was out of the hospital, in more of a "home-like" environment (though it wasn't like our own home). Gregg and I could sleep in the same bed; we could kiss our children "goodnight" and tuck them in, relax in more privacy than we could in the hospital, and talk as a family, without staff members interrupting due to the hospital's schedule. We were together as a foursome, instead of two and two.

We met others who were in similar situations, and we began to develop new routines, based upon the requirements of the day. At least 4 nights a week, dinners were provided for residents of the House, free of charge, due to the generosity of various volunteer groups. There was often an activity planned for the children, and sometimes free tickets to local events were offered to families.

In order to stay at Ronald McDonald House, families pay a minimal amount (we were also paying our mortgage, taxes and other bills for our home). Thanks to the generosity of the donors to Ronald

McDonald House, we were able to make this move. Because Gregg's employer offered excellent medical insurance for its employees, every penny of Katie's medical care was covered in full, and for that, we will always be grateful. These two provisions relieved a great deal of stress on us.

> *We did not want to put Katie through the agony of treatment, if she was going to die no matter what the doctors tried*

When Gregg and I first became aware of what we were facing - when the doctors said Katie could die any minute - we discussed all that was said, and decided that we did not want to put her through the agony of cancer treatment if she was just going to die at the end of it. We felt it was too harsh, and that it was a bad way to spend the rest of your young life at the age of 11; we were in complete agreement about that.

One of our good friends, Diane Fuquay, M.D. (who was also our children's pediatrician) had recently died after seven years of metastatic breast cancer. We loved Diane very much, and saw a lot of cancer's effects through her journey; she had a stem cell transplant, and she suffered a great deal, taking it all with heroic grace and fortitude. Our children saw Diane when she was very sick - and just before she died - and they knew a bit about what cancer could do. We did not want to put Katie through the hell of treatment, if she was going to die no matter what we tried.

In the case of a child, when you speak with experts – the only people who know what you are facing – when they offer hope, and your child wants to live as much as you want her to live, you grab onto that hope. So we accepted the doctors' recommendation that the *only* chance she had of surviving was to take the chemotherapy. They gave us hope that she would make it through the treatment, to have surgery to remove the tumor. If the surgeons could not remove the tumor, it was obvious that Katie was going to die, because it had already taken over her adrenal gland, kidney, part of her liver, filled her inferior vena cava and entered her heart.

Around this time, we received good news: Katie's scans showed that the blood clots (or tumors – it was never clear exactly what they were) in Katie's lungs had been dissolved, either by the blood thinner (given by injection twice a day) or the chemotherapy treatments! This was a sign that things

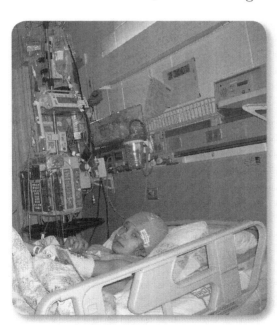

Katie inpatient, receiving IV medications, November 2006

were improving - perhaps the chemo was already doing its work. This gave us hope that, in the long run, the treatment could have the same kind of effect on the larger tumor. Even though Katie was suffering, seeing improvement like that made me feel that this might be worth it. And chemotherapy was the *only way out of this*, for Katie; surgery was not an option, yet.

As Katie survived each round of chemo, I would visualize the tumor being attacked by the drugs. I suggested that she think of the chemotherapy drugs as a liquid form of love and intention, created and delivered by the researchers, doctors, lab technicians, drug companies, nurses, and so on. I told her that everyone associated with the chemo wanted her to get well; it was like a bag of their prayers and intentions for her healing. She may or may not

> *It gave us pause to know that what we were doing to try to save our child's life could also possibly harm her, in the long run*

have accepted that, but it comforted me to see it this way, and I hoped that it might strengthen her will, and her belief in her own potential for healing.

After a child has been treated with chemotherapy, she needs to be checked for certain side effects, because different chemo regimens can create different damaging effects. One of the potential side effects of Katie's chemo was hearing loss, so she went to a specialist in the hospital to have her hearing checked. Fortunately, she had no hearing loss at that time, but it gave us pause to know that what we were doing to try to *save* our child's life could also possibly impair her health in the long run.

We saw many children on the ward who had trouble walking, or talking, who were deep in rehabilitative therapy because of the effects of surgery, or the side effects of radiation and chemotherapy. It's torture for them, and for their parents to witness the suffering. Some children will be unable to have children of their own in later life, due to the effects of their treatment regimen. These are huge issues that we didn't think about in Katie's case, until it was staring us in the face on the treatment consent forms!

I used to think about the fact that the drugs were toxic - that if Katie didn't have cancer, we would go to jail for poisoning her. The nurses would come in wearing gloves and a big apron when they administered the medication that was going directly into my child's bloodstream. It is so corrosive that they can't touch it with their bare hands, but it's going directly into your child's body, right near her heart…it horrified me, when she would use the toilet and her urine came out bright red (she was not bleeding; it was a side effect of the medication). It was hard to watch our child suffer – for example, vomiting seven times a day creates worries about her hydration and nutrition, in addition to her discouragement and discomfort.

Witnessing such painful, distressing indignities which a cancer patient goes through, day in and day out, is wearing on the family. As adults, we can take the long view - we assume that her hair will grow back, she will get strong again, her appetite will return, food will smell and taste good again – someday - but to a child, even the wait between Halloween and Christmas seems long. They live in the present, and for a child in a cancer ward, the present is awful.

Enduring five rounds of chemo takes a long time, and it wore Katie down emotionally, as well as physically. She became very frail; she had to use a wheelchair, she had scars and bruises on her arms and legs from all of the daily injections. Her skin didn't heal as it normally would have. Her abdomen grew distended; her skin developed a gray tinge.

It was my privilege as her mom to help Katie when she took a bath, and this routine continued at Ronald McDonald House. She was a private girl in some ways, but she let me help her with this. Cancer patients are susceptible to feeling cold, so I always tried to keep her cozy. It was an opportunity to give her a treat, a bit of a "spa" feeling. Sometimes, she would ask questions and talk about serious topics, such as, "What if I die?" That is where she preferred to talk about her fears – when she was soaking in the bathtub.

When Katie first began to introduce these subjects, I wanted to reply, "Let's not go there; you're doing well, and we need to focus our energy on hope." I discussed this with our Childlife worker, Julie, who told me that that was not the right approach to take. She said that if Katie wanted to confide her fears in me, the best way to deal with it was to let her say anything that was on her mind. She told me that I needed to be a "safe" person with whom Katie could share all of her thoughts, including her fears.

Even though I didn't want to think about the possibility of Katie dying, I needed to let her think about it, and talk about it. After that conversation with Julie, I would listen and discuss whatever Katie wanted to talk about. We never, ever misled or lied to her about her situation.

One day, Katie and I were walking around the hospital, and we went to a family sitting area where there are comfortable chairs, books and magazines, computers and a nice view. The late actor Christopher Reeve's wife, Dana, had recently died of lung cancer - she had no history of smoking, and that was a big topic in the news at that time. Seeing it on a magazine cover, Katie and I were talking about that, and I said I thought that she had really died of a broken heart, because she and her husband were so close, especially during the 10 years of his disability (after his riding accident). I told Katie that I didn't think Dana Reeve wanted to live without her husband. Katie said to me, "Mom, if I die, don't do that." I really wanted to reply, "Let's not talk about that," but I knew that was not the best way to respond to Katie's words on this sensitive subject, so instead, I said, "You're doing well. I have a lot of hope for you, but if it happens, okay, I'll try not to do that."

> *It's a good idea to pause before entering our room, and take a moment to breathe, because we might be in the midst of a sacred or painful conversation*

That was a painful moment, when I simply had to stay present; I had to stand up, in spite of the pain, and be the person my daughter could rely upon. When a doctor, a technician, a nurse, a chaplain, a janitor or anybody comes into a patient's room, they have no idea what kind of conversation or moment they are walking into. It's a good idea to pause before entering our room, and take a moment to breathe, because we might be in the midst of a sacred or painful conversation like that one.

Ronald McDonald House is an educational place to live – it's a melting pot, filled with all types of families from diverse backgrounds, from all over the Northwest, with every kind of socio-economic, educational, and financial history. The House turned out to be a much better place for us to live than the hospital. David had a tendency to complain that he had to "sleep on a bench" (the long, padded window-seat which was designed for use as a bed) and he argued with us over our requests that he do our family's regular House chores, but other than that, he tried to make the best of the experience in every way possible. I used to joke that we were on "a really horrible vacation in a pretty nice motel." We were deeply grateful for the accommodation.

David attended school with cancer patients and their siblings. He would come home and tell us interesting stories about how people interacted, and what he had done during the day. Though the school day was short, much was accomplished, and the variety of subjects and activities was enriching. He immediately moved into this community where he knew no one, and adjusted very well, but it was not easy for him.

David developed skills at entertaining himself, and gradually became more independent. He found that the gourmet grocery store next to Ronald McDonald

House made tasty smoothies and sandwiches, which he enjoyed eating as his school lunch or snack. He would have benefited from more parental attention, but under the circumstances, it was simply impossible to give him what he was used to having at home. This led to my feeling torn and guilty, but I had to simply do the best I could each day.

For his birthday, David asked us to take him to the restaurant at the top of the Space Needle for dinner. Because Katie was still an inpatient at the time, it took many months for us to grant his request. Eventually, Gregg was able to take David up to the restaurant there, and I stayed in the hospital with Katie. I ordered a special cake for him, with an edible tennis court on top of it, to celebrate his first year on the high school tennis team. We did our best to help entertain David, but there is no denying that it was a hard time for him.

It was fascinating to see the coping skills of the various families; for example, one group of people cooked a great deal. The last thing I wanted to do at that time was cook – Katie could barely eat, and I couldn't eat much, either – yet here were these beautiful people, cooking traditional dishes from scratch, and nurturing their family with food. It was eye-opening.

Once, in the middle of the night, Katie awoke to find that her feed pump had come unhooked from her NG tube; it had pumped formula into her bed. This made the bed wet and smelly, so she woke Gregg and me, and we changed her sheets. David slept through this, though we had to turn on the lights in order to change the sheets.

Suddenly, I heard a racket out in the hall - loud yelling and swearing – so I went to the door to look out of the peephole. As I peeked out, a naked woman streaked down the hall, holding on to what looked like a bedspread, swearing at the top of her lungs. She opened a door and ran into the dining area.

I assumed she was one of us – the mother of a patient, who, under terrible stress, cracked, and ran screaming out of her family's room, without her clothes. Gregg and I continued changing Katie's sheets, turned off the lights, went back to bed and to sleep.

When we got up in the morning, we found out that she was *not* one of the residents; she was a person who had a mental illness, and lived down the street from Ronald McDonald House. For some reason, the House security guard had let this woman in, in the middle of the night. I had glimpsed her on the run through the house, screaming obscenities and tearing quilted decorations from the walls.

> *Intense stress was so much a part of our daily life that I felt we were all just one small degree away from craziness.*

What I find most interesting about this is the fact that I had assumed she was *one of us,* because I could easily understand it happening. That assumption told me a great deal about where we were, emotionally - intense stress was so much a part of our daily life that I felt we were just one small degree away from that kind of craziness - all of us.

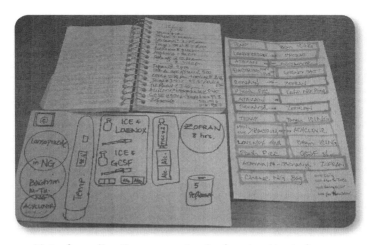

List of medications on a typical outpatient day

After each remaining round of chemotherapy, Katie was released from inpatient to outpatient status. At Ronald McDonald House, Gregg and I got the medical routine under control, but it was a very complex assignment for a layperson. Because I was afraid that we might make an error and jeopardize Katie's health, I had to create a reliable system. I drew diagrams and lists to keep everything organized, and I kept a daily log of every single thing that happened - how many cans of feeds Katie took, if she threw up (how many times and about how much came out), her temperature (morning and evening). If Katie's temperature rose above a certain point, we called the charge nurse and discussed whether we needed take Katie back to the hospital. That happened a couple of times, and that was a great disappointment, because Katie preferred being out of hospital.

During Katie's treatment, different family members would take turns coming to Seattle once a week, and frequently brought dinner for us so that we had something to eat other than hospital food or Ronald McDonald House meals. Often, they would stay with the children so that Gregg and I could go out on a date and speak to each other privately over a quiet meal. That turned into a very helpful routine – about once a week, Gregg and I would go out to dinner.

People in our community were generous, donating gift cards or money to help us to be able to afford to do this. I believe it helped our marriage - and our sanity. It's forbidden to drink alcohol at Ronald McDonald House and the hospital, for good reason, so to be able to eat a quiet dinner together, and perhaps drink a glass of wine, to speak to each other privately, looking into each other's eyes and just being a couple, was a great treat. We were rarely alone during Katie's

Once a week, Gregg & I would go out to dinner. People in our community were generous, donating gift cards or money to help us to be able to afford to do this. I believe it helped our marriage - and our sanity.

treatment - we had no privacy, and all of the stress and worry are hard on a marriage. Those dinners on our own helped to relieve some of the stress, and provide an opportunity for communication and intimacy.

At a certain point during her treatments, Katie didn't want me to be out of her sight. One night, when my parents were at Ronald McDonald House with her and David, she asked them to telephone me and Gregg at the restaurant. My parents complied, and told us, "We didn't want to interrupt you, but she wants to talk to you," and they put Katie on the phone with me. She started to cry, saying, "I miss you; I want you with me." We were at a restaurant only about two blocks away, and were in the midst of dinner, so I told her we would be back soon. We hurriedly finished our meal and returned to the House.

It hurt my heart to hear Katie crying and saying, "I miss you." She was normally a very independent girl, so this was an example of regression, due to the stress of having cancer. Childlife told us that this was a common occurrence, under the circumstances. There were other signs of regression, such as in her taste in TV shows: Katie began to enjoy watching cartoons that would typically appeal to younger child. She liked reading "Peanuts" comic books, and liked to have me read Nancy Drew mysteries to her.

At Christmas time, my sister took David and me out on a Saturday while Gregg stayed with Katie. We bought little artificial Christmas trees at a craft store, along with ornaments and decorations, because no real trees, plants or flowers are allowed on the cancer ward. We gave David and Katie each a tree to decorate as they wanted. Katie was not very excited about it. However, I helped her decorate her tree, and we put both of them up in the room at Ronald McDonald House.

Carolers came to perform for us in the living room at the House, with a fire in the fireplace and cider and cookies provided for all, but Katie didn't want to leave our room to join in the fun. Everyone around us did the best they could to bring the feeling of Christmas into the situation, but being in treatment for cancer threw a huge damper on everything for Katie. We were unable to inspire her to participate in any festivities.

In December, we were allowed to go home for the first time in over two months. Katie was thrilled to be in our home, to see our cats and to sleep in her new double bed, in the privacy of her own room. We all slept well and felt refreshed. While we were at home, there was a windstorm, and our power went out; because we have a wood stove, we were cozy. Our neighbor has a generator, so he charged Katie's feed pump, enabling her to have her liquid nutrition. It might sound difficult, but it was so good to be together at home that the inconvenience didn't matter – we played games by firelight and candlelight, and just enjoyed the peace and beauty of our home. Going home gave us renewed energy, alleviated some of our homesickness, and it gave me more hope.

On a different trip home, we were waiting in our car on the ferry dock. We had a special pass that allowed the ferry staff to give us priority on the boat. This meant a spot near the restrooms on the car deck, and quicker loading on (and unloading off of) the boat. David was terribly homesick at this time (as all of us were), and was desperately anticipating and in need of this break. We were waiting at the head of the line when Katie began bleeding heavily from her nose (a common side effect of cancer treatment, indicating low platelets). Gregg and David were in the front seats, and I was in the back with Katie, when she slumped over in her seatbelt and said, very quietly, "I'm done. It's got me." I thought at that moment that she was going to die. I knew that a nosebleed is normal under the circumstances, but her response to it was so far from normal for her, that it frightened me.

I said, "Honey, you are exhausted; you just need platelets. You have a nosebleed, and when we get this under control, you will be fine." I told Gregg that we needed to turn around, go back to Ronald McDonald House and call the hospital, and ask them to order platelets for Katie. David protested; he was terribly disappointed, and we were so close to home! However, we couldn't go on with our planned visit home; it would be too risky to get on a ferry for a 35-minute ride, with Katie's nose bleeding profusely, not knowing if or when we could get it to stop. I was wiped out emotionally, hoping that Katie was not going to give up.

> *In that moment in the back seat of our car with Katie, I wondered, "Is this it?" and was terrified that she was going to give up and die, right then and there.*

In that moment in the back seat of our car with Katie, I wondered, "Is this it?" and was terrified that she was going to die, right then and there. My next thought was, "How can I help?" I wanted to help her to feel safe and hopeful, to know that this nosebleed situation was temporary, and that she had a remedy waiting for her, back at the hospital. I also felt awful for David, whose disappointment was understandable and legitimate. Gregg and I were disappointed and homesick, too, but we couldn't give way to those feelings.

Gregg drove us back to Ronald McDonald House. We settled Katie into bed, telephoned the on-call doctor at the hospital and told him what had happened. He was calm and helpful. They ordered blood products for a transfusion the following day. Katie's nose stopped bleeding, and we took her to the hospital in the morning, where they infused her with platelets. She looked and felt much better after that, so they let us go home. Though her nosebleed cut the weekend visit short by one night, it was just a part of the package with cancer treatment. We appreciate the blood donors so much for their gifts of life!

When David complained about his hardships and disappointments during this period, I used to say to him, "I am sorry about this, and all that you are going through and missing, but *she's on fire*; you're not. I hear your unhappiness, but you will have to wait. We have to put out the fire right now." To his great credit, he did a wonderful job of dealing with his frustrations constructively. He did not complain often; he had to wait for, and give up, a lot of things he wanted to do. He was always completely supportive of Katie, and did his part to help us with her. David was always a delight to us and a loving brother to Katie; he matured beyond his years during this family crisis.

Mouth sores are a side-effect of chemo, and Katie had to be admitted to the hospital for a fever and excessive vomiting in between rounds of chemo, due to mouth sores. It took a little bit of diagnostic discernment to discover that her "mouth" sores were in her throat; her NG tube was irritating the sores in her throat, stimulating her gag reflex and causing vomiting. Once she was hospitalized, Katie was able to have a patient-controlled anesthesia unit to help her manage the pain, which stopped the irritation and vomiting. Katie also developed skin issues, with bruises and scabs from the many injections which were not healing, so she was visited by the Dermatology team.

She began to be quite antisocial, which was very much out of character. Katie had been a social person all of her life, making friends everywhere she went, yet at that point, she didn't want to see any of her friends. She tolerated family visits, but would not meet other patients if she could avoid it, and never reached out to befriend a roommate. She stopped keeping in touch with most of her friends back at home, and prohibited me from making any connections for her with other children on the ward.

Katie was facing huge issues, with the tumor itself, all of the treatment and side effects, and a possible surgery in the future, not to mention the worries that come with a cancer diagnosis.

There was further deterioration of her moods, and I thought, "We need to get her on an antidepressant." I had been resisting that, because I thought that once a person starts taking an antidepressant, it can be difficult to stop using it, and in any other situation, I would have tried counseling and other resources first. We didn't have that luxury, at this point - she did not want counseling - so I asked for whatever medication was appropriate for her.

The first response to this request was the return of the Psych team. Different people came, one at a time or in pairs, and after the third person came to interview her, Katie looked at me again with an "Are you kidding me?" expression. I went out into the hall and found the attending physician.

We knew each other well by then, so I said frankly, "I think we both know that that exercise was a failure. *You* know she needs an antidepressant, and *I* know she needs an antidepressant. Can we please get this done?" Dr. Matthews kindly took care of it, and Katie started taking Prozac. It helped; while it didn't make her cheerful overnight, it did help her establish a baseline of moderate happiness.

> *I said to the doctor, "I think we both know that that exercise was a failure. You know she needs an antidepressant, and I know she needs an antidepressant. Can we please get this done?"*

On some days, I felt trapped - in a sense, "locked up" - in the room with Katie at Ronald McDonald House. Gregg would go off to work in the morning, and David would go to school, and I felt stuck in that dark, basement room, a bit like a prisoner, while Katie preferred to watch TV most of the day. In the midst of a long winter, I started to feel like climbing the walls; not enough daylight, not enough human contact, not enough exercise, too much worry and stress all combined to weigh heavily on my heart.

> *At times, I felt trapped...this is not the life we were used to; it's not the life that we would like to give to our children, and it's not a path we have chosen.*

One day, I left the room briefly to telephone my best friend, and said, with deep sarcasm, "If she wasn't so sick, I'd kill her!" This was the only friend to whom

I could have said that, and she laughed hard and understood - she didn't judge me. That was a relief. I went back into our room and said to Katie, "I miss seeing people; I feel lonely here when you don't want to see anyone." She said, "I didn't say YOU couldn't have people over. *I* don't want to have people over!" That was a bit of a breakthrough, but it's difficult to keep four people in one small room together, in bad circumstances.

It's important for all of those who help us, whether it's Childlife, doctors, nurses, chaplains - to try to understand what the worry, stress, responsibility and lack of freedom feels like to us, day in and day out. Even in outpatient care, this is not the life we were used to; it's not the life that we would like to give to our children, and it's not a path that we have chosen – we were forced to be here through a health crisis. We have no choice but to take this journey – a journey which no one wants to take.

David with family in Poulsbo, Christmas 2006

We talked to David about how he would most like to spend the holidays, and he felt that he would have a happier holiday if he spent Christmas at home with our extended family, since Katie was in the hospital, finishing a round of chemotherapy. He went to Poulsbo and celebrated Christmas with his aunts, uncles and cousins, staying a few nights with them.

Katie spent Christmas Eve in the hospital, taking her last doses of a week of chemo. We brought her little artificial Christmas tree into her room, with its decorations and lights on, and I spent the night there with her. Gregg slept at Ronald McDonald House, and came to the hospital on Christmas morning. Santa visited during the night and brought lots of presents for all of the patients. One of our favorite nurses was on duty that night, so that made it better.

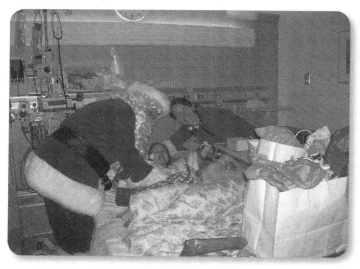

Katie with Santa & Nurse Shauna, Christmas day, 2006

On Christmas Day, the staff wanted to let us out of the hospital as early as possible, but Katie wanted to stay, until she had all of her anti-nausea medications infused through her PICC line. She knew that she was going to feel sick when she got out of the hospital from the chemotherapy's side effects, and the IV medications seemed to work better for her, so we spent about half of Christmas Day in the hospital.

When we moved back to Ronald McDonald House, some of our family came to be with us. The same wonderful group that had prepared Thanksgiving dinner came and made Christmas dinner for all of us.

CHAPTER 4:

A New Year, with Hope

*I*n early January of 2007, Katie had been through the chemo cycle four times. Her chemotherapy was always administered while she was an inpatient, so that meant five days in the hospital (if there were no complications) and then returning to Ronald McDonald House for about 3 weeks of recovery. We developed our outpatient routine: in the morning, Gregg would get ready for work and David, for school. Gregg would take David to the hospital to catch a shuttle to the Hutch School, and Gregg would drive to his office. In the afternoon, David took a shuttle back to the hospital and walked to Ronald McDonald House, and Gregg would join us a couple of hours later.

In general, we didn't have to wake up during the night to take care of anything, but from early in the morning until bedtime, there was a complex medical schedule to follow, and a written record to be kept of everything that happened during the day. I'm a visual person, so I actually traced the outline of all the equipment we used (vials, thermometer case, bottles of pills and liquid medications, heparin syringes, etc.) and wrote the name of each item in its outline, and that helped me to keep everything organized, and prevented mistakes. I always worried that, as an amateur nurse, I might forget something, which could jeopardize Katie's health or her recovery. It was a huge responsibility for a parent who had no prior medical experience. As we practiced this routine, it became less terrifying, but it took up a large part of my day and my thoughts.

When Katie was re-admitted to the hospital for each round of chemotherapy, she decided that she preferred to have Gregg and me taking care of her needs, over the nurses, which was a big surprise to us. We did everything that we were allowed to do, from changing her bed's sheets to administering shots, helping her to the toilet, the tub, ordering food from the kitchen, getting warm blankets for her, etc.

During the weeks when she was in outpatient care, Katie had to go to the Hematology-Oncology Clinic twice a week for a blood draw and basic examination. The staff would weigh and measure her, and check her "labs" (information drawn from her blood) to monitor her progress after each chemo cycle, as she was coming out of the neutropenic state. Each round of chemotherapy takes a huge toll on the immune system – its effects are cumulative – so, later in the cycle, we spent a lot of time doing very little, as Katie grew progressively weaker, more nauseous and fatigued.

Eventually, she didn't feel like going anywhere, so we spent most of our time in our room at Ronald McDonald House. Eating was prohibited in the individual rooms at the House, so when I needed to leave the room to eat, I took my mobile phone with me so that Katie could always reach me. When we were all together, we took turns leaving, so that someone was always with Katie, and she didn't feel abandoned. In the early days, Katie would sit with us in the dining area of Ronald McDonald House and try to eat, but later, her sense of smell became too sensitive, and she lost her appetite. That lasted for months; even after she finished all of her chemo cycles, she did not enjoy eating. That was a sad side effect; eating is a natural, universal human need - a source of pleasure, a part of life and culture everywhere, and her cancer treatments robbed her of that.

The trips to clinic twice a week were an ordeal, because in between chemotherapy cycles, Katie felt weak and nauseous. Just the *thought* of going back to the hospital triggered nausea, and she would gag and vomit before we even left our room at Ronald McDonald House. It was very difficult to motivate her to get out of bed, change her clothes or put something on over her pajamas and get up and go outside to the car. I would start the process early, as gently as possible, because there was no way around it - clinic appointments were a medical necessity. I felt terrible for Katie, because I would not have wanted to go to the clinic, either, but there was no way out of those appointments.

We would begin with Katie's anti-nausea and anti-anxiety medications, and then she would sit up in bed, and I would help her to dress. She would move to the edge of the bed, and then she would start to gag and be sick. I would clean her up, help her refresh herself, wash out the pink bin, and then we would slowly make our way to the car (with the pink bucket). I would drive up to the hospital doorway, get a wheelchair and settle her into it with her quilt, and park the car as close to the door as possible. Then I would wheel Katie into the clinic. Sometimes, Gregg helped me take Katie to the clinic before he went to work in the morning, and sometimes David assisted us, because it was difficult to transfer her to and from the car on my own. Sometimes, Katie would receive a Beanie Baby at her appointment, and in the early days, that made her happy, because she collected them, but as she got progressively sicker, even that didn't help.

My brother and sister-in-law enjoy skiing. They gave David a package of beginner's ski lessons as a Christmas gift. David went up to Snoqualmie Pass with them for his lessons, and he loved that; he developed a passion for skiing that continues to this day. It was a wonderful gift for him, to get into the fresh air and out of the city, to exercise and take his mind off of the situation back in Seattle.

My sister took David shopping. He took fieldtrips with his class at the Hutch School, and had the opportunity to meet professional athletes and experience a variety of good things that would not have been available to him through his school at home. He attended sporting events, and was a guest in luxurious private box seats, which he enjoyed enormously. Those days out helped relieve the boredom and tedium of hospital life for David.

I love Seattle Children's Hospital and their way of delivering family-centered care, and am especially thankful for the fact that we never had to send Katie alone into an experience that was upsetting or frightening to her. For certain scans, they provided lead aprons for moms and dads to wear; I could hold Katie's hand through most of the scans and procedures. She

> *I am thankful for the fact that we never had to send Katie alone into an experience that was upsetting or frightening to her.*

was allowed to take her quilt everywhere she went in the hospital. In the echocardiogram room, there was a video player, so Katie would lie on the exam table wearing a hospital gown, and the technician would check her heart, while Katie and I watched "The Princess Diaries." That movie will always be associated with "echoes" at Children's Hospital, in my mind.

I appreciated the fact that, for every movement Katie had to make - ultrasounds, MRI or CAT scans, X-ray - I could always be with her. It gave me great comfort to be of service and comfort to her. I couldn't make the cancer or the horrors of treatment go away, but I know that having someone present with you, who loves and cares for you, is helpful.

I learned this from Katie, when I made her attend the hospital school, early in her treatment regimen. I insisted that she try it, because I wanted her to live in the assumption that she had a future – that she was going to get out of the hospital - and because of that, continuing her education was important. I believed that it would help her to meet other children, to keep up with her class and age group, but she did not want to do this, and she fought against it. Because this was early in her chemo regimen, her nausea was hard to predict - she wasn't very sick during her first round of chemo, though it got progressively worse with each cycle.

On that day, Katie gave in to me, so Julie from Childlife escorted us to the fifth floor classroom; we took Katie in a wheelchair. As soon as we got to the door of the classroom, Katie vomited. She looked at me miserably, as if to say, "You made me do this; I told you it wasn't a good idea." At that moment, I felt terribly guilty for making her do something she didn't want to do, but I also knew that my reason for pushing her was for her long-term benefit. I knew that chemotherapy caused sickness, and that sickness was not my fault, but my heart went out to Katie.

We cleaned her up, took her back to her room, and requested anti-nausea medication for her. Later, she asked me, "Do you know what I was thinking when I was feeling so bad outside of the schoolroom?" and I told her I didn't. She said, "I kept thinking: Mommy loves me; Mommy loves me. Mommy loves me," and it helped. I remember that, because even though I had forced the issue of school that day, apparently, my presence still meant comfort to her - and that comforts me.

By the end of January, all the scans and tests were done, and the information was submitted to the surgeons. We waited to find out whether they thought it was possible to remove Katie's tumor. We also considered if we had choices to make regarding where Katie should have the surgery. Would it be safest here in Seattle, where we knew the oncology staff? Or should we look into St. Jude's hospital, where the protocol for Katie's kind of cancer had been designed? What would give her the best chance of survival? Would it be too difficult to travel with a child who was so fragile and sick? How would we arrange lodging and support?

After considering all of the questions, we decided to stay in Seattle. We felt we needed all of the family and community support that being near our home would offer. Moving that far away, even temporarily, would take too much out of all of us. Katie gave her opinion with her own brand of humor: "Travel to Memphis? I'm not having my surgery where ELVIS lived!" Though we had nothing against Elvis Presley or his music, Katie made it clear that Tennessee was much too far to go, and the association with Elvis just went against her preferences.

Katie's oncologist conferred with the surgeons who she felt were the best suited to performing such a delicate operation. They are two of the top doctors in their fields: Dr. John H.T. Waldhausen is the division chief of general surgery at Seattle Children's Hospital, and Dr. Gordon A. Cohen, the division chief of cardiothoracic surgery.

They took time to review her progress, and the changes which had occurred as a result of the five rounds of chemotherapy Katie had endured. The surgeons determined that it was worth the risk to try to remove her primary tumor. They met with Katie,

Gregg and me first, and then, alone with Gregg and me, and explained their plans.

The surgeons allowed Katie to ask questions. She asked, "While I'm in surgery, can you please pierce my ears, so that I won't feel it?" I loved how the doctor took the question seriously, and answered, "In another situation, I'd be happy to try to do that for you, but I think it won't be a good idea during this surgery - so I have to say 'No.' " Katie was disappointed, but she accepted that. Then she went out of the room with our Childlife and Social Worker, and we discussed the nitty-gritty with the surgeons.

> *They could not promise us that she would live through the surgery, which involved removing her left adrenal gland, left kidney, a lobe of her liver, and her inferior vena cava.*

They showed us Katie's scans, and told us how intricate, far-reaching and dangerous the procedure was going to be. They said, in effect, that they could not promise us that she would live through the surgery, but that they were going to try to remove her tumor – all of it. That also meant removing her left adrenal gland, left kidney, a lobe of her liver, and her inferior vena cava. I don't remember what we asked, but I do recall Dr. Cohen expressing confidence. He said, in effect, that he had never had anyone die while he was performing surgery, so that was comforting to us. We knew that surgery was the only way out of the situation, for Katie.

Even after chemotherapy, her tumor had not shrunk; it was still widespread throughout her abdomen, encasing those two organs, and invading her liver and heart, interfering with her blood flow. She could not live with the tumor in her body; it was a threat to her life, every single day. Surgery was the only way to give her a chance to live her life without that threat - so Gregg and I gave our permission, and the surgery was scheduled for February 21, 2007.

We were allowed to go home for three weeks, from the end of January into February, so that Katie could rest, recover from her chemotherapy and enjoy being away from the hospital. It was the longest we'd been at home since October, 2006, and it felt more like normal family life. Not that this was *normal*, because Katie still had cancer, and was awaiting a huge surgery, but it was certainly better to be in our own home.

Because Katie's immune system could not handle water drawn from a private well, we had a special water-filtration system put into our kitchen to protect her, and we used a lot of hand sanitizer. Surrounded by the loving care of friends and family, eating our own food, enjoying one another's company, having our own rooms and thus, a bit of privacy – all simple pleasures that one might take for granted - was heavenly, for us. It felt very luxurious. We had to give up our room at Ronald McDonald House so that another family could use it while we were at home, so we packed everything we had there, and brought it home with us. The House could not guarantee that a room would be available when we needed to move back for Katie's surgery, so we put our name on the list, waited and hoped that we could move back in when the time came. Meanwhile, we enjoyed living in our own environment.

Katie at home with Maribeth, January 2007

Katie's pre-operative appointment was scheduled a few days before her surgery. I drove her and a friend of the family onto the ferry and over to the hospital. We sat down in an exam room, and I noticed that our friend was looking at Katie's arm. There was a big blood stain on her sleeve – blood was seeping through it - and I stared at it, in shock. Fortunately, our friend had medical training, so he grabbed some towels, applied compression to Katie's arm and calmly suggested that I call for the nurse.

When the nurse arrived, we realized that Katie's PICC line had sprung a leak; the plastic tubing had developed a crack. The decision was made to simply pull the PICC line out then and there, because Katie was finished with chemotherapy. That was good, but

I had nightmare flashbacks afterward about what might have happened if it had sprung a leak sometime in the night. We could have awakened to find Katie with blood all over! If it happened without a trained medical professional on hand, it would have been much more frightening. I still feel anxious when I recall that appointment. I was profoundly grateful that our friend was with us when it happened, and that he knew exactly what to do.

Katie was prescribed an antibiotic cream which was to be rubbed at the opening of her nostrils each day, just before the surgery. We were aware that we needed to guard her health very carefully always, but especially in the days preceding her surgery; I was on edge about this.

In honor of Valentine's Day, Gregg and I made reservations at an elegant, quiet restaurant near our home. We set out to enjoy a romantic meal in the nearly-empty dining room, only to have an obviously sick man seated at the table right next to us. As our table neighbor repeated a deep, productive cough over and over again, I told Gregg that we would have to ask for a different table, but he did not want to do this; he felt it was unnecessary and embarrassing. I couldn't relax and enjoy our dinner, because I was terribly concerned that one of us would catch the bug from our neighbor, pass it on to Katie, and cause her surgery to be postponed. Against Gregg's wishes, I asked our waitress if we could move. After we were seated at the new table, away from others, I thanked her and quietly explained the situation. She was very sympathetic; however, the evening was ruined. That is a small example of the sort of marital stress with which we lived.

Before Katie's illness, we used to watch PBS mysteries (we still enjoy them). The night before we moved back to Ronald McDonald House – two nights before Katie's surgery - all four of us were in Gregg's and my bed, watching a PBS mystery, and unfortunately, as the plot developed it became apparent that a part of the story involved some characters trafficking in live donation of human organs - selling a kidney on the black market, to make money. I had never even thought about that subject, let alone discussed it, and wouldn't you know, it came up in the movie we were watching that night.

I began to worry about Katie watching this episode, since she was about to have surgery, so I said something like, "This is just a story – it's not like that." Katie replied, "Well, I am not going to have a kidney removed," and there was complete silence in our room. She said it again: "I'm not going to have a kidney removed, *right*?" to which we replied, "Actually, you are."

She became very intense and said, "Why didn't you TELL me I was going to have a kidney removed?" We reminded her that she had made it quite clear that she didn't want to know about her surgery – she didn't like us to discuss it in front of her. She said, very strongly, "I think I would like to know if I'm going to have a KIDNEY removed!" She was going to have much more than just a kidney removed, so we asked her what else she wanted to know, and answered her questions. A very uncomfortable subject (and timing) of a TV show, to say the least!

The next day, we loaded the cars and moved back into Ronald McDonald House. A room was available for us, and this one was not in the basement, which was an improvement, because it received more natural light. We got settled, and for fun (and distraction), we drove to a toy store near the hospital and bought a huge Playmobil gift for Katie – the Modern House. The children spent the evening assembling this house and everything that goes with it; it was a superb activity for the evening before surgery. That helped to keep our minds somewhat occupied.

A friend had recommended a prescription for Xanax for me, so it was filled, and on the night before Katie's surgery, I took the first Xanax I'd ever had. He described the medication to me as a muscle relaxant; he said it would help me to sleep the night before the surgery - it is not habit-forming, so I didn't have to worry about that. I took one that night, and one in the morning on the day of Katie's surgery, following the directions. It did help me to sleep, and it gave me a reasonably calm feeling when we took Katie to the hospital for her surgery. I appreciated the suggestion.

On February 21, 2007 - which happened to be Ash Wednesday – we took Katie to Seattle Children's Hospital for her surgery. David took the day off from school, and Gregg from work. We arrived at the hospital around 7:00 A.M., as we were instructed to do. Our beloved Childlife worker Julie met us there. We knew that this was a very risky surgery, but we also knew it was the only way for Katie to have a chance to live, so we felt a combination of great hope and anxiety. As parents, we didn't want to communicate our anxiety to our children; we did our best to communicate hope, calm and faith that she was going to come through it.

Katie and I went into a dressing room together so that I could help her change out of her clothes and into a surgical gown. She was given medication to help her relax, and she appeared to be calm. We were allowed to stay with Katie until she was called into surgery, and it was easier to let her go because Julie, our Childlife worker, went with her to the operating room.

> *It was helpful and comforting to see Katie go to her surgery with someone we knew, someone with whom she was at ease, and who she trusted.*

It was helpful and comforting to see Katie go to her surgery with someone we knew, someone with whom she was at ease, and whom she trusted. We kissed our daughter goodbye, said "We'll see you later," and she left, in the capable hands of loving staff. We were given a pager, and were told that we would be contacted with updates every couple of hours.

We walked around the hospital all day long. We must have eaten meals, but I don't remember any of that. Friends and family came to wait with us. Many people were praying for Katie that day, because they knew that this was a big surgery. Our church community, friends, extended family and acquaintances all around the world were praying with Katie and us. A group at the University of Washington held a prayer vigil; people gathered, not only in our church but elsewhere, to pray for Katie. We knew that the whole day was held with loving intention, prayer and hope, and that gave me comfort and endurance through the hours of waiting.

After a couple of hours, we were paged, so we found a "house" telephone, called the number, and were told, "It's going fine. They are just getting in," and about every two hours after that, we were paged and told that they were still "getting in" – in other words, it was going slowly.

I noticed a lot of people around the hospital with a little smudge of ashes on their foreheads, as is customary to do on Ash Wednesday, and I remember thinking, "There is no way I'm going to put ashes on my forehead today! This surgery is enough of a sacrifice."

Going into such an experience - whatever your spiritual framework – will test what you believe. On my spiritual path, I had been taught that the Holy One is the Parent of all things - the Creator. I believed that the Holy One knew my heart as a mother, and that everything that was happening to Katie was held in that knowing Love. I felt instinctively that I didn't have to tell the Creator of the universe what was going on – I trusted that it was known, and so I took in all of the loving intention and prayer wholeheartedly, and with great gratitude. *I had to let go,* because I had to trust the process. There was nothing more I could do; I was not driving the bus, so to speak. We were present with love and intention for Katie's healing, and that's all we could do. It was the longest day of our lives.

Eventually, night fell, and Katie was still in surgery. Having started around 7:30 in the morning, it was a long day without much information, in spite of the pager buzzing every couple of hours.

We learned later that Katie's circulatory system had made many other pathways for her blood to flow around the tumor, and that the reason it had taken so long to operate was that the surgeon had had to painstakingly open her body around all of these other blood vessels, in order to get to the tumor as safely as possible.

At around 11:00 P.M., we were paged again, and this time it was a call to come down and meet with the thoracic surgeon. Gregg and I went to see him in a private room, and Dr. Waldhausen said words to this effect, "Dr. Cohen is working on her heart right now, and when he's done, I'm going to start on her liver. It is possible that she will die during that part of the surgery."

> *I will always love that surgeon for taking the time to bravely tell us this terrible news, face to face, with seriousness, composure and compassion*

We were stunned, because Katie had been in surgery for so long, and all of the updates had made it sound as if it was going fine. They hadn't given us a lot of details, but what we had heard indicated that she was stable. I remember crying and asking him, "Why now? Why would she die now, after she's been okay for all of these hours?" He said, "When I cut into her liver, there will be a lot of bleeding, and I think she may bleed to death."

I will always love Dr. Waldhausen for taking the time to bravely tell us this terrible news, face to face, with seriousness, composure and compassion. He had done most of the surgery up to that point; he could have been resting, perhaps eating, and taking care of himself. He had the strength of heart to face us and prepare us for the worst news a parent can receive. He could have spared himself this unpleasant task, but he knew that we would need preparation for such a blow, so he told us personally.

We staggered back upstairs under the weight of this news. We shared it with the few people who were still waiting with us. They called other friends and family members and asked them to pray. I tried to pray, and I must have dozed off, because the next thing I remember is that the pager awoke me. Gregg and I rushed downstairs, and this time, we met the cardiac surgeon, who was all smiles. He told us, "My part went great." He had been able to reach in, and pull the tumor out of her heart. We learned from him that it had not embedded itself in her heart; it had entered it, but was not attached, enabling his part of the surgery to go smoothly.

We were stunned by his happiness, because we were not expecting good news, at that point. What joy, to find out that she was still alive! He told us that Katie was doing fine when he finished his work, and that Dr. Waldhausen was now working on Katie's liver. We went back upstairs with renewed hope, shared the good news with our companions, and continued to keep vigil.

At 4:30 in the morning, we were paged again, and told that Katie was being taken to the Cardiac Intensive Care Unit, and settled into her room. The surgery had taken 18 hours, and they had saved

Katie's life. They said we would be able to see her in a few minutes. It felt like a resurrection – to have her back from the brink of death. I have never been so relieved and happy to see anyone as I was to see my daughter, when we were allowed into her CICU room in the early morning hours of February 22nd, 2007.

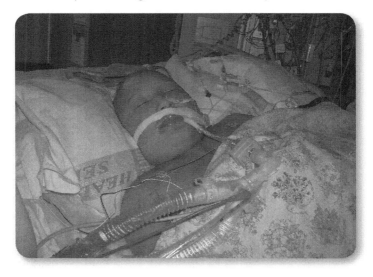

Katie in ICU after surgery, February 2007

When we were taken to see her, Katie looked different from anyone I had ever seen before. She was terribly swollen – she had used 70 units of blood products, and completely wiped out the supply of her blood type at the Puget Sound Blood Center. It was frightening to see her, because no one had prepared us for how different she would look after such a long surgery.

All of her hair, eyebrows and eyelashes were gone; her neck was barely visible. The worst part, for me, was the fact that the surgeon hadn't been able to completely close her incision, because she had taken on so much fluid. There was a HUGE scar from the hollow of her throat past her belly button, and from side to side – like a cross – closed with stitches, and, at the center of that cross, the

> *No one had prepared us for how different Katie would look after her surgery*

incision was covered only with a dressing. It troubled me terribly that they couldn't stitch it closed, but it was impossible at the time, due to the amount of her swelling.

There were drains everywhere – big, bubbling surgical drains, large plastic boxes with thick tubes, attached to her body. She had a catheter, a new PICC line, a thick nasal cannula, and several smaller drains; she was intubated and had many lines and wires on her body, attached to monitors. It was shocking, but we were thrilled, because she was ***alive!*** That's when I began to believe that Katie was going to live and recover from cancer. I thought, "She came through that surgery; prayers have been answered. She's getting a second chance to live without that f*cker (my private name for her tumor) in her body!"

Dr. Waldhausen told us that he had removed the entire tumor, with clean margins. The surgeons originally thought they were going to have to remove and rebuild Katie's inferior vena cava, but her body had created alternate pathways for her blood flow while the tumor was blocking her IVC, so they didn't need to build a new one. Rather than rebuilding it, they made a connection using her pericardium. The fact that Katie's body had made other paths for the circulation of her blood at the same time that the tumor was growing, undetected, is a miracle of the human body. That miracle gave me hope for her recovery and healing.

CHAPTER 5:

The Road to Recovery

Katie's surgery took place on February 21st and lasted into the early hours of the 22nd. Shortly after the surgery, our church held its annual Women's Retreat, and Maribeth told me, "Everyone is asking about you. Do you want to me to tell them anything at the retreat?" I replied, "Please thank everyone for their prayers, and tell them that if they want to do something to help, they can donate blood to the Puget Sound Blood Center. Katie used all of her blood type during her surgery, and it needs to be replaced." As a result, there were three separate blood drives held on Bainbridge Island in Katie's honor.

Immediately following Katie's surgery, while she was in the intensive care unit, we were not encouraged to sleep in her room. I feel uncomfortable about that to this day. Katie's CICU room was one of the smallest in the unit, and though there is a place for a parent to sleep in each room at Seattle Children's Hospital, this particular room was arranged in such a way that we couldn't pull out the parent bed in order to make it up. We noticed this when we first saw her after her surgery.

> *Immediately following Katie's surgery, we were not encouraged to sleep in her room. I feel uncomfortable about that to this day.*

We could have asked the staff to move Katie's bed and all the supporting medical equipment (which was large, with some attached to the walls and some free-standing). That would have made extra work for them, and I suspected that they may have arranged the room that way intentionally, knowing that we would not get much rest in the ICU. Katie's ventilator made noise, and her drains were bubbling; there were bright lights and activity around the clock in CICU.

Another reason that we allowed ourselves to go back to Ronald McDonald House to sleep at that time was the fact that we had a pager. Ronald McDonald House is less than five minutes away from the hospital. I made the nurses promise always to wake us if there was the slightest reason to come back. I received the impression that the staff felt it would be better for us, in the very first days after Katie's surgery, to get as much sleep as we could – which meant sleeping elsewhere. No one said anything overt, but the impression was there.

Dr. Waldhausen came to examine Katie, as he often did when she was recovering in the ICU, and said, "She is still very sick." I remember being fearful at the potential for infection, knowing that Katie's organs were somewhat exposed, since her incision was still partially open. It had been closed as far as possible at the end of her surgery, but the center of the incision was not yet stitched closed. That was very shocking and uncomfortable to my sensibilities as Katie's mother. I kept asking, every single day, "Can they close it today?" but for many days, it was impossible, as she was still retaining a great deal of fluid from the surgery.

I can't adequately describe how much the thought of that open wound (covered with a dressing, but not closed with sutures) troubled me, every day. It made me feel more nervous about her already-precarious health. The surgeon had to use a special material to close the place where Katie's scar formed a "cross"

> *I can't adequately describe how much the thought of her open wound (covered with a dressing, but not closed with sutures) troubled me.*

in the middle of her abdomen, and that material's delayed arrival had pushed the surgery back an extra day. After waiting for 12 days, Katie's swelling had reduced enough so that the surgical staff was finally able to fully close the incision on her abdomen. Once Katie's incision was closed, I was able to relax a bit.

I took a Xanax every day for a week or so following Katie's surgery, because it was very harrowing to see her in her post-operative condition; I also took it at night to help me go to sleep. I felt guilty and uncomfortable every night when we left the CICU to go to sleep at Ronald McDonald House.

Gregg, seeing how stressed I was, made it clear that he felt that I needed to sleep at the House so that I would get enough rest to make it through each day. In order to deal with my ambivalence about being away from Katie at night, I told him and the nurses that as soon as Katie was awake enough to notice my presence or absence at bedtime, I would immediately move into her room.

For the first couple of weeks, Katie didn't know day from night; she was on many medications for pain (as well as amnesia-inducing drugs) and she slept most of the time. The nurses promised me that Katie would never remember any of that period, and so, although I was unhappy about it, I allowed myself to be persuaded to leave her each night from about 9:00 P.M. until about 7:00 in the morning. Fortunately, Katie had no crises while I was at Ronald McDonald House during the night. That would have been a nightmare scenario, to be away from her when she needed me, but it never happened.

Because Katie was so fragile and sick, we decided not to allow anyone to visit her in the CICU other than Gregg, David and me. I knew that the sight of her, unconscious, with all of the tubes and equipment attached to her, would terrify my parents, so I told them not to come. My best friend is the only one who I allowed to come in to see Katie – she has had several surgeries of her own, and is unafraid of hospitals. Yet even she broke into tears right away – it was hard to see someone you love looking so very ill.

During this time, some people in the hospital contracted a stomach virus, and the ICU was even more restricted than normal. We all had to wash our hands twice before entering the ward. At that point, the staff tried to discourage David from coming in to see Katie, but we overruled that as politely and firmly as possible. There was no way that I was going to keep him away from his sister. Even if she was unconscious, and he was only allowed into her room for a few minutes a day, he needed to see his best friend and have some contact with her.

The CICU is a very technical part of the hospital and the staff is highly trained. Even with all of the nursing that we had done up to that point, I did not have the training to deal with her condition after surgery. I'd like to emphasize what a helpless feeling I had in the ICU, at first. To see Katie in that state, and not be able to help her, was terribly stressful.

We had wonderful nurses, and a couple of them stand out. One of them completely understood how I felt, and taught me a number of things that I could do to help Katie, such as massage lotion into her feet or her arms. I brought a scented lotion that Katie liked so that she could feel my loving touch, and take in the good smell with her senses. This kind nurse showed me how to use a special sponge-toothbrush with water to brush Katie's teeth; I applied lip gloss to keep her lips moist and comfortable.

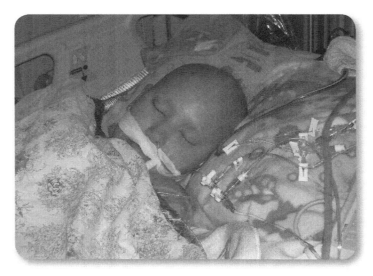

Recovering from surgery in ICU, March 2007

At first, it didn't seem as if I should ask how to help, because Katie was so fragile that I was concerned that my inexperience and ignorance might hurt her. I also didn't want to bother or distract the nurses, who are specially trained professionals with many years of experience. As we got to know one another during the many hours we shared by Katie's bed, I found the courage to ask the nurses what I could do, and they very kindly and cheerfully taught me.

As a mother, the desire to help when your child is badly hurt is so powerful that I would say it is *unstoppable*. I wanted to take her in my arms, cover her and protect her, take away the pain, take her home – at the very least, I wanted to climb in bed with her and comfort her, but there was no way to do that, because there were tubes and lines connected to her all over her body. I wanted to get my hands on her, to help her get well, bring comfort and soothe her - and the nurses wisely understood this. They taught me how I could contribute to Katie's care in a

> *As a mother, the desire to help when your child is so badly hurt is very powerful –*
> *I would say it is unstoppable.*

way that would help, and not hamper their work.

It was therapeutic for me to spend every day with Katie, and to learn even more about rounds in the ICU. Once I got over the shock of seeing her in this state, rounds were of great importance for me, because Katie was intubated (her breathing was being done for her by a machine), unconscious and couldn't speak up to advocate for herself. Surgical drains, arterial line, a cannula in her nose (that came from her stomach to drain bile, because she wasn't able to digest), catheter - I wanted to learn what all of that paraphernalia did for her, so I tried to absorb everything I could.

Did I need to check the tubes, telling the nurse when a drain or the catheter was getting full? What were the machines doing, what did the numbers on the monitors mean, and what were we looking for as to her progress and healing? BUN, creatnine, SATs and the like were all new to us, so I put my energy into learning what the numbers meant, what we were looking for, what meant progress and what indicated a problem.

I don't know whether all of the doctors appreciated my intense interest, but if you look at it from my perspective you will see that I was Katie's advocate, the closest person to her, the one who knew her from the moment of conception, and she was my child, my responsibility. I needed to know all I could in order to help her get well. This gave me a healthy focus for my energy, and it kept me busy in a positive way.

In the CICU, the ratio is one nurse per patient. Each morning, the night nurse would prepare her report to hand over Katie's care to the morning shift. I would arrive around 7:00 A.M. and check in with the nurse before rounds began (at about 7:30 A.M.). I soon learned what was reported each day, what were the goals in Katie's healing, what they were following and what was of most concern that day.

The group at rounds would include Katie's nurse, me, the attending physician and the other teammates (usually the fellow, residents, students or other doctors). I could ask questions, and I learned to offer input on certain things, especially if I felt strongly about an issue. I'm not a doctor; they were the medical experts, but there were some things (such as the timing of pulling Katie's catheter out and putting her on a bedpan) about which I did have a reasonable opinion, and I was heard.

> *It was important to me that my input was respected, because I knew Katie, and was thus able to advocate - to "mother" her - even while she was unconscious in the ICU. It made me feel much less helpless, less restless, and more useful.*

It was important to me that my input was respected, because *I knew Katie*, and was thus able to advocate - to "mother" her - even while she was unconscious in the CICU. It made me feel much less helpless, less restless, and more useful. This lowered stress in parents is likely better for the patient, as well as the medical team.

At times, fluid built up in or around Katie's lungs, so that would have to be removed. When she needed x-rays, the staff was able to bring the machine up to the ICU to avoid moving her when she was so weak.

After a major surgery like Katie's, we had to be very patient and wait while her body healed. We could pray for her and deal with our stress internally, but for the most part we had to watch and wait. I can't say strongly enough what a blessing the nurses were in helping me through all of it. They were compassionate, supportive, kind, fun, loving and calm.

Katie and I have always loved looking at family photos, so I made posters using photos of Katie, healthy and in her "real life," doing things she loved with family and friends, to display in her hospital room. We took them with us each time we went in for a round of chemotherapy, and it was a good way for staff to get to know Katie and our family. The posters also helped to start conversations when new people arrived on staff. We put those up on the sliding glass doors to her CICU room. Before anyone came into Katie's room, I wanted them to see photos of her, whole, healthy, active and doing all the things that she loved, so that they wouldn't look at her as simply a sick person. I remember thinking, "This is who she is, and this is where we're going - back to this; you need to hold this vision in your mind, and help us get there."

When she was unconscious in the CICU, I brought Katie's baby book from home, to give me something else to work on with my hands. One of the nurses noticed what I was doing, and brought colorful paper for me to use. This is another example of the tender, family-centered care which the nurses provided for us.

Katie's birthday is March 8, 1995, so I had a "birthday countdown" on the door to her room, and every day I would change the number so that everyone would know Katie's birthday. I was hoping that she might be conscious and able to enjoy her birthday. One of Katie's favorite nurses changed her schedule so that she could be Katie's nurse on her birthday.

Another of the nurses, who shares Katie's birthday, came in to see her (even though it was her day off), and brought presents to Katie. That touched me deeply, and I will always remember her kindness. We hung colorful lanterns in the room, I made birthday posters, and we celebrated as best we could, but Katie was not awake most of the day.

While she was unconscious, Katie did some funny things. I came in one morning and found the nurses laughing. When I asked them what was so funny, they told me that they had had a little excitement with Katie during the night. They said to her, "The next time you decide to pull your arterial line, let someone know!" Apparently, in her drugged state, she had yanked out one of the lines from her artery – a sudden move, which caused a lot of bleeding. The nurses had it under control, but that would have upset me, if I had been present – an example of another reason not to sleep the CICU at that time! The nurses thought that Katie was hilarious.

When she was intubated and still deeply sedated, Katie managed to roll over in bed, well before the nurses thought she would be able to do so. That was a good sign, to me, that she was getting stronger and that her independent character was again asserting itself.

She had to wear a leg brace, which looked like a boot, on one leg at a time to prevent "foot drop." It was easy to see that she hated it. Even though she was sedated and intubated, Katie was told by her nurse, "If you can flex and point your foot a few times now and then, we won't have to put the boot on. Can you do that?" and then she helped Katie practice this move. Soon, Katie was able to exercise her foot by herself.

Even while she was sedated, she was responsive, and able to do things that surprised me. Unfortunately, she also experienced hallucinations; she would point to the lights in the ceiling and look worried. I asked the nurses, "Do you know why she is doing that?" and they said that Katie indicated to them that she saw blood dripping from the ceiling. I asked them how they could tell what she was saying while she was intubated, and they said, "We just know" – they are accustomed to interpreting such things. It upset me to think that Katie was having nightmare visions and was unable to understand what was happening to her. The nurses repeatedly assured us that Katie's medication would wipe out all of these memories, but it was troubling to see her suffering.

One of the funniest things that Katie did while intubated occurred when her nurse was watching the computer screens and monitoring Katie from outside of her CICU room. She could see Katie through the glass doors, just a few feet away. Katie – still intubated and hooked up to many drains and monitors - was suddenly sitting up on the edge of her bed. She had her legs over the side, so the nurse went in and asked her, "What are you doing?" to which Katie shrugged her shoulders, indicating, "I can't say." The nurse pursued it: "Are you trying to get out of bed?" and Katie nodded "Yes" – caught in the act!

We were taught that every time she woke up in the CICU, we should always tell Katie, "You're doing great; your surgery is over, and you're recovering now. You're in the ICU, getting better." We did this every time she woke up. One time, when she was still intubated, she woke up, and I said, "Hi sweetie - you're doing great…" and the whole story, yet again. Katie furiously mouthed the words - around her breathing tube – "I *KNOW*!" and she started to pull on the tube, as if to take it out. I said, "No - you can't take that out - it's there for a reason – it will come out when you're ready," and she looked at me very angrily and mouthed, "I'M *READY*!" She was feisty and asserting herself, even while she was heavily medicated. That made me happy, because I could see she was in there, and was getting stronger if she could be so expressive, even with the breathing tube in place. One of my friends said she could just imagine Katie's irritation as we told her the same thing, for what must have seemed like the 100th time, assuming that she couldn't remember it – when in fact, she could.

The respiratory therapists worked with Katie, and when she was finally able to be extubated and breathe on her own, she was less sedated and spent more time awake. Her voice came back, and she was able to watch TV and movies once again, and to interact with us more.

One evening, as I was going back to Ronald McDonald House, I said privately to the nurse, "I think she's going to notice that I'm gone tonight, so if she says one word to you, *please* call me - I'll come right back to sleep here." As soon as we got into our room at Ronald McDonald House, the phone rang, and it was Katie's nurse. She said, "She asked for you," so I quickly put my things into a bag and went right back to the CICU, and walked into Katie's room, as casually as possible, as if I'd just been to the bathroom. The nurse told me privately that, as she was getting Katie ready to go sleep for the night, Katie said to her, "I'm not going to sleep yet, because my mom's coming back; she always sleeps here." By this time, the staff had rearranged Katie's room so that I could pull out the parent bed and easily make it up. That night and always afterward, I slept in the hospital with her, until she was discharged. It felt so good to be with her at night again; though sleep is difficult in a hospital, I hated being separated from my girl.

Once Katie's tumor was removed, pathologists conducted more tests on it, and confirmed that it was in fact adrenocortical carcinoma, as Dr. Park had suspected. We knew then that they had treated her for the right thing during the last four rounds of chemotherapy. We donated Katie's tumor to the National Tumor Bank, which keeps samples of tumors so that they can be used by any doctor or pathologist who is trying to diagnose a disease.

The staff asked us if we wanted to see photographs of the tumor. I said, "Yes, I do." They gave us copies of the photographs, which were taken after it was removed from Katie's abdomen.

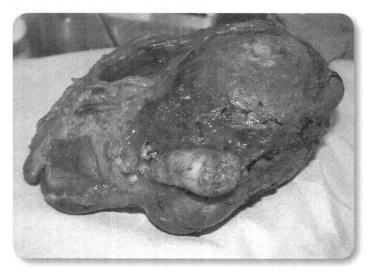

Adrenocortical carcinoma tumor, after resection from Katie's abdomen

It's a horrible-looking thing; part of it looked like raw meat, or some kind of roast, to me - I couldn't eat meat for a while after that. It had absolutely consumed Katie's kidney and adrenal gland, and her inferior vena cava looked like a sausage casing, full and bursting open with tumor.

It was good to be able to focus my anger and hatred on that "f*cker," and to know that it was no longer inside of her, causing trouble. I felt that she now truly had a second chance at life. That was a very positive and hopeful feeling, after worrying daily for months that the tumor might kill her.

We were advised (initially, when Katie was diagnosed) not to do a lot of computer searching, because the material on the internet is not filtered; there is a great deal of misinformation along with good information, and we wouldn't have the knowledge to discern between what was true and untrue. I have to tell you, though - everyone does it – and in the beginning, everything we read was bad, so we decided to step away from searching online.

The hospital generously provides books about pediatric cancer to parents, and maintains a Family Resource Center, but the books available had nothing whatsoever on Katie's cancer. It was not even mentioned, it's so rare; the protocol wasn't written up in any of the materials we were given, and we could not find survival rates. We got our information from Katie's oncologist, and she got the treatment protocol from St. Jude's Hospital - the only hospital in the country that was studying this very rare tumor at that time.

However, after Katie survived her surgery, we did indulge in more online research, since we had a conclusive diagnosis. Everything we found told us that she was at stage IV, and it was all dismal, bad news and terribly discouraging. We began to wonder if we had done the right thing, putting her through the chemotherapy and surgery, when all that we read online suggested that patients with her kind of disease (a "non-performing tumor"), as advanced as her case was when it was discovered, would be dead within an average of 9 months. The doctors had found microscopic bits of tumor in the part of Katie's liver that they had removed, and we knew that was a bad sign. Gregg and I began to feel quite discouraged, but we kept our feelings private, between the two of us.

Katie's surgeon, Dr. Waldhausen, was checking on her progress one day, and when he came out of her room, I told him that we were feeling discouraged – that we were concerned that we had put her through all of that agony for nothing. He drew a little diagram of Katie's surgery for me and said words to this effect: "I got clear margins; I think you have reason to hope. We've been very aggressive up to this point, and you don't want to give up now; I think we need to continue to be aggressive."

That meant a lot to me, coming from him. He has a quiet, serious demeanor – he is not the type to sugarcoat communication - and when he said that to me, it strengthened my hope, and gave me enough fortitude to face what was in front of us, and to continue the course.

The oncologists told us that Katie's accumulated chemotherapy would continue to attack the cancer in her body, even after she had finished receiving it. They planned to start a follow-up regimen of oral chemotherapy (in pill form), after she had recovered from the surgery, so we were not out of ammunition. The drug (called Mitotane) was the only one that had been shown to be effective against recurrence of ad-renocortical carcinoma.

I grew close to the staff in the CICU. There were small, silly things that some of us found we had in common, such as a mild "addiction" to office products. One day, I went for a walk to a nearby office-supply store and bought a few of my favorite pens to give to those staff members who I knew shared that interest.

There were also moments of shared humor which made us feel at home in that ward. For example, David was studying the circulatory system at the Hutch School, and he had an assignment to draw a poster with a diagram of it. Because part of Katie's surgery had been on her heart, she was in the Cardiac Intensive Care Unit, and while David was working on this project, he showed his poster to some of the staff and asked them if it looked right. One of the attending physicians was hilarious about it, and said to another, "I think he [David] is smarter than you are." They were ribbing each other and including David in the fun, and that sort of thing helped us to bond with them.

One of the doctors was quite funny, saying such things as "The day I got married, my dad told me, "Son, you can marry more money in a day than you can earn in a lifetime!" I had never heard that saying before, and it made me laugh.

These little moments add up; they help us to form

> *These little moments add up; they help us to form a relationship that goes beyond doctor-patient-family member, to a real connection as human beings.*

a relationship that goes beyond doctor-patient-family member, to a real connection as human beings. Seeing each other as individuals with a history, a family and a life beyond the hospital, gave depth and strength to our relationship that took us beyond Katie's illness, yet helped us to care for her more effectively. We formed a team, working together to alleviate her pain, to help her to heal and get out of the hospital - and back to her childhood.

It may sound strange, but I have happy memories of the CICU, because I loved the staff. They helped me to endure the strains of Katie's illness, and to grow while doing so. I learned to advocate for her more clearly and strongly, and grew in understanding medical terminology, body systems - to be able to "sling their lingo"- as an essential part of Katie's team. It was extremely rare to have a staff member talk down to us; most accepted that we were the experts on our child. That is another example of family-centered care, and it made an enormous, positive impact on how I felt while enduring a very difficult time.

> *I have happy memories of the CICU, because the staff helped me to endure the strains of Katie's illness, and to grow. I learned to advocate for her as an essential part of Katie's team. That made an enormous, positive impact on how I felt while enduring a very difficult time.*

After three weeks in the ICU, Katie was well enough to move to the surgery ward.

This was huge progress, because it meant that she was going to start to be ambulatory - to have therapy, to gradually be weaned off of the surgical drains, and to grow stronger. The move to the surgery ward was also welcome because it was a less-restrictive environment than the CICU.

One of the nurses in charge of the surgery ward read Katie's chart and noticed how much she had been through, so she assigned Katie one of the greatest rooms in the hospital. It is a private room, with a huge northwest-facing window in an L-shape, which brings lots of light into the room. Cherry trees were in bloom in the neighborhood, and we could see them through the window; it was lovely, on gray days, to look out and see those pink blossoms. The room had a private bath with its own toilet and shower, and I was allowed to use this, because Katie could not use it (in the beginning of her stay). It was wonderful to stop going to the 5th floor to take a shower, and to have a private toilet.

The surgery ward had a different atmosphere from the other wards. To refresh your memory: we had started in the ER, were admitted to the cancer ward, moved to the intensive care unit, back to the cancer ward, went home, then into the cardiac intensive care unit, and now we were on the surgery floor. We met new residents, doctors, fellows and nurses, and embarked on a new learning curve as we adjusted to how things work in that ward. There was a simpler medication schedule than on the cancer ward; there were fewer machines than in the ICU. Katie's day was far less scheduled, so I began to consider what she could constructively do with her time, other than watching TV and videos, or resting. I requested physical therapy for her, and asked the nurses for ideas as to what was appropriate for Katie to be doing at that point in her recovery, to keep her motivated and hopeful.

Katie finally felt well enough, after she moved to the surgery ward, to look at her birthday presents and cards. Because she had slept through most of her birthday, she opened cards and an abundance of presents with pleasure and surprise as if it was the real day.

March is also the month of my father's birthday; he turned 80 that year. He did not want to have his birthday party without Katie, but a family member persuaded him to at least go out for dinner, so Gregg stayed with Katie, while I went to the party with David and the rest of the family. It was hard on everyone, because we missed Katie and Gregg, and my dad didn't feel right celebrating without them, but he did his best to be appreciative.

My parents have three grandchildren, and two of them are boys; Katie is the only girl, and the youngest. My dad had a special relationship with her, and when she got sick, he wanted to do anything he could think of to inspire and encourage her. He said, "I want to take everybody on a cruise for my 80th birthday, but we are not going until Kathryn can come, too." We found a beautiful brochure for a cruise line - small cruises, around 200 people per ship - and so we began to dream about that trip, planned it and thought about what fun it would be, when the time came.

There were times when Katie had to leave her room to have a scan or test. The staff would bring a wheelchair for Katie, help her into it, and hang her remaining surgical drains on the back of the wheelchair. She still had two big tubes attached to her body that led into large drains, and a few smaller ones, each of which ended in a small bulb. Moving around required help and planning.

Our wonderful physical therapist, Linda, and her colleagues came to help Katie work on flexibility and strength. Because her incision went from the hollow of her throat down past her belly button, and from side to side, with a large intersection in the middle, she had a huge number of stitches and was stiff and sore, with a lot of mobility issues and a great deal of scar tissue.

In order for Katie to get stronger and return to her old life, doing what she used to be able to do, she would to have to be patient and work at her therapy. The first thing was to sit on the edge of the bed; as she got stronger, Katie got off the bed, stood up and then sat in up in the easy chair which was a couple of feet away from her bed. Next, she took a walk around her room; after that, she walked down the hall, and eventually, she took laps around the ward. It was a great gift that the physical therapists had known Katie since before her surgery, so they had a good relationship; that made it easier for her to respond to them, but therapy was hard work. She was still very weak from the surgery and the weeks of lying unconscious in the ICU.

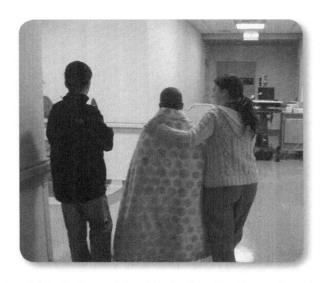

David & Katie walking the halls with Nurse April in March, 2007

Every day, the team would arrive in the morning for rounds (around 7:00 or 7:30) – the attending physician and all of the residents - perhaps a dozen people. I was dressed and ready to go, and they would appear at Katie's door, asking if they could come in.

> *Rounds began with questions such as, "Have you passed gas today?" Now, imagine a beautiful, 12-year old girl facing this question from a crowd of strangers.*

According to Katie's wishes, I would allow the fellow or the attending physician to come in - the residents would normally stay in the doorway, behind a privacy curtain, so that they could listen to the conversation. Katie did not feel up to facing a crowd of "strange" people, first thing in the morning.

Rounds began with questions such as, "How are you this morning? Anything new since yesterday?" and then, "Have you passed gas today?" Try to imagine a beautiful, 12-year old girl facing this question; she did not want to discuss that issue with a crowd of strangers, so she occasionally pretended that she was asleep.

One of the things I appreciate about family-centered care is the way the staff speaks to the patient – they never talked over Katie's head, but spoke directly to her. They *never* ignored her to address us, as if she wasn't present; staff was always respectful of Katie, but at times, she didn't

> *One of the things I appreciate about family-centered care is the way the staff speaks to the patient – they never talked over Katie's head, but spoke directly to her.*

want to participate in discussions. If that was the case, Gregg or I would be her spokesperson - but we always allowed her the right and the responsibility to speak for herself.

Katie's digestive system wasn't "awake" at this point; she wasn't passing gas and she wasn't able to take in nutrition except through her IV (using TPN, or Total Parenteral Nutrition), which was the reason for the team's daily questions on the subject.

Until she could digest food, even liquid food through her NG tube, Katie could not be released to go home. She was frequently nauseous, throwing up bile. Eventually, I could tell it was coming – I would watch the automatic pump that was supposed to be drawing off the bile into a container, and if it was moving too slowly, I would detach it from her NG-tube, attach a big syringe to her tube and draw the bile out of her stomach with the syringe and dispose of it. If I didn't do this soon enough, she would begin to look ill (or tell me she wasn't feeling well), and would then be sick to her stomach.

The team decided to find out if there was a blockage somewhere in her system, because after surgery that is a possibility, so they ordered a scan. This is what I remember as "one of the worst scans, ever." We had to slowly pump barium dye into Katie's NG tube – an opaque, pinkish liquid which shows up on the scan. Unfortunately, she had to take in quite a lot of it. I hated doing this to her, because I knew that she was probably going to throw it all back up, but they had to put a certain amount into Katie's digestive system, in order to get a good image on the scan.

We took her in a wheelchair, and when we got to the scan room, found that I had to get Katie out of the wheelchair, up onto a high table and lying on her side. That was difficult to do, as she was nearly as tall as I am. It was uncomfortable for her, and the room was cold, so I tried to keep her warm using her quilt. Once on the table, she started to throw up the barium dye. It was at that point that the staff told me that the scanner was not working! I felt rather angry at that.

It wasn't anyone's fault that the scanner quit working, but I was upset that we had pumped Katie's stomach full of dye, got her out of bed, hoisted her onto an uncomfortable table in a cold room, only to have her get sick - and on top of that, to receive no information from it!

All of her discomfort, as frail as she was…to this day, it makes me queasy to remember it. In my frustration, I told the staff, "If you want to take another one of these scans, bring whatever you need down to our room; we are not coming back here to do this again! She is much too frail for this." That is one of my worst memories - of needless suffering. I knew that the scan was ordered to gather information for Katie's well-being, but I wished there was a better way to obtain it, without causing nausea, vomiting and so much suffering to her. Once her digestive system began to function, Katie tried drinking juice and smoothies. When she could tolerate them, her NG tube feeds were gradually resumed.

Seattle Children's is a wonderful teaching hospital, and as parents of a patient, we agreed that the staff should be able to learn from our experiences. In theory, we did not mind being part of their educational process, but because Katie had been through so much by this time, I felt especially protective of her. There were certain things that I did not want the residents to do; I felt that she deserved a fully-fledged, highly-experienced doctor. Having her stitches removed was one of those things.

> *There were certain things that I did not want the residents to do. I simply felt that she had been through so much that she deserved a fully-fledged, highly experienced doctor.*

When the time came to remove some of the stitches from Katie's enormous abdominal scar, I was told that a resident was going to come and do the job. I said, "I don't like that idea; I want the surgeon." I was told that he was busy in the operating room. I replied, "That's not a problem; we'll wait. When he's ready, we'll be here." So we waited, and one of the fellows, who had assisted with Katie's surgery and knew her, arrived to take the stitches out.

I appreciate the fact that I was able to voice this request, and to have it granted. The scar was so large, so long and wide, and looking at it brought back the trauma of her surgery - the fear, and the precariousness of Katie's health. It gave me comfort to have a doctor who was familiar with her history removing the stitches.

Our Hematology-Oncology Childlife worker shared some "tricks of the trade" with Katie, in order to make the removal of her stitches and drains easier. This kind of care is crucial to helping patients feel less fearful and more empowered.

Our Hematology-Oncology Childlife worker, Julie, came to the surgery ward and shared some "tricks of the trade" with Katie, in order to make the removal of her stitches and drains easier. She coached Katie through these new experiences. The value of this kind of care is hard to fathom, unless you have experienced it. It's not common, everyday knowledge, and to have this kind of "inside" information shared when it is needed is crucial to helping patients feel less overwhelmed, less fearful, and more empowered.

On a lighter topic: some people love clowns, but Katie and I were not fans. Gregg and I took the children to *Cirque du Soleil* when they were small, and some of the performers came into the audience, which upset our children. None of us in the family were clown-lovers, and, in the hospital, sometimes professional clowns come to entertain the children. They knock on the door to a child's room, come inside and perform their clown act. For children who enjoy them, I'm sure clowns are a welcome diversion. Katie was not one of those children.

The clowns that we met often had terrible timing, arriving just when we were trying to take a nap, or unhappy about something – precisely at a time when we didn't want one more stranger coming into our room. It got to be so irritating that I actually drew a cartoon of a clown with a red circle and a slash through it, and stuck it on the outside of the door to Katie's room: "No clowns allowed."

In spite of this sign, one day a clown entered the room while I was napping and woke me. Irritated at the interruption of my rest, I sat up halfway in bed, looked at her - she was in full clown regalia – and said, "Didn't you see the sign? We don't want clowns to visit." Her reply is still memorable: "Oh! We don't have to be clowns!" I thought, *Of course you are a clown - just look at you! You're dressed like a clown - you're wearing the outfit, clown shoes - what else could you be?* That

> *Privacy is rare and precious in a hospital, and it is important for staff to respect it, particularly volunteers.*

exchange disturbed me, because it seemed that her need to perform took precedence over our need for privacy (and to be "clown-free").

Privacy is rare and precious in a hospital, and it is important for staff to respect it, particularly volunteers.

Blood Drive, March, 2007

Three blood drives were organized in our community to replace the 70 units of blood that Katie had used during her surgery. Someone had a huge banner made, which said, "Blood Drive Dedicated to Katie Gerstenberger," and it was posted alongside of the highway, next to one of the hosting churches. It was seen by thousands of people who commuted to the ferry every day on that highway. My father took a photograph of the banner, and sent it to me in an email; I showed it to Katie. She didn't register much interest in it, even when I told her about the blood drives being held in her honor.

A drive at our church was scheduled for March 30, and - to my surprise - on March 29, Katie said to me, without warning, "Get me a pass; I want to go to my blood drive." Even though she had appeared to be disinterested when I told her about it, she clearly took in the information and decided that she wanted to be a part of the event.

We asked for the doctor's permission to go out for the day, and received a pass. Though Katie was still very frail, she was happy as we got into the car and rode the ferry across Puget Sound to our church. A friend had a wheelchair waiting for Katie, so she didn't have to walk, and we wheeled her into the blood drive.

The event was held where we used to take part in youth group meetings - a familiar part of the church - and people were thrilled to see Katie. We were touched and inspired, because they were all giving blood in her honor. This was the first time in five months that many of them had seen Katie. Taking this "fieldtrip" wore her out, but it also made her feel good. It brought up feelings of homesickness in me, because we were so close, yet we had to return to the hospital; it was a tantalizing glimpse of what we were missing.

The blood drives were hugely successful; they took in more blood than Katie had used in her surgery, and many new donors signed up. Those who can give blood are literally saving lives; Katie would never have lived through her surgery if there had not been a blood supply available to replace what she lost, so we are deeply grateful to all blood donors.

CHAPTER 6:

Home!

Just before Katie was released from the surgery ward to come home, her surgeon, Dr. Waldhausen, came to see her. Katie was never warm and cozy with her doctors, but this one - who she knew had done the lion's share of her surgery - she liked very much. After he had finished examining her, he sat and talked for a bit, and suddenly, she said, "We're going to have a party to celebrate when we get home - when the weather is warmer - and I'd like you come." He said he would like that.

Another day, after he checked on Katie's progress, I went outside to the hall with him to speak privately for a moment. I said "I've been wondering: Katie has a huge amount of scar tissue on her stomach, and you had to use special material to close the center of the incision; would she ever be able to have a baby? What would happen to her abdomen - would the skin be able to expand enough to accommodate a baby?" I don't remember the words he used, but he gently assured me that it was possible.

I remember looking into his eyes and thinking, *This must sound crazy to him*, but I was thinking about

> *I remember looking into his eyes and thinking, "This must sound crazy to him," but I was thinking about Katie's future.*

Katie's future. Most important, of course, was her survival, and after that, her fulfillment as a human being. She loved little children, and she might want to have a family, and I was worried that the scar tissue from her life-saving surgery might prevent that. Dr. Waldhausen could have treated me as if I was crazy, thinking so far ahead in Katie's life, but he didn't – and I'm thankful for the way he handled that moment.

At that time, we had not yet addressed what the chemotherapy might have done to her reproductive organs, because she hadn't fully entered puberty. We didn't think about harvesting her eggs, and it is possible that she was too fragile to consider that step when she was first admitted to the hospital. Nowadays, the issue of fertility is addressed with the adolescent and young adult population, if possible before treatment begins - if the patient has time to consider it. Katie was 11 1/2 when she started treatment, and her reproductive future hadn't even crossed our minds - until after her surgery.

On April 1, 2007, Katie was discharged from the hospital for good. What a great day that was for all of us! We packed our cars and drove to the ferry. I can't quite describe the joy we felt. I was thinking: *We did it! We escaped - we got her out of there, and we're going HOME!*

Now Katie could get stronger, in the comfort of her own room, surrounded by familiar things, in the fresh, salty air of home. She could put the hospital experiences behind her, and rebuild her "real" life. It was not, by any means, back to "normal," but Katie had survived everything that was thrown at her - she had taken treatment, survived surgery and recovered with her valiant spirit - and it was a positive move, to be in our own home again. David and Katie were free to go back to playacting and video-taping each other, playing video games and board games, enjoying our woods, the rope swing, etc.

Unfortunately, Katie still suffered from severe digestive problems when we moved home. She was free to eat what she wanted from a medical stand-point, but she still had to use liquid nutrition to get enough calories, as her appetite had not returned. That meant that she had to be attached to the NG tube feeds through a portable pump, which she carried in a little backpack. We charged the pump each day, and generally ran her feeds at night, so that she could be free of the pump during the day. While she could sit up with us at the table during meals, she had very little appetite and her sense of smell was still hyper-sensitive. Although we wanted her to join us at mealtimes, it was very difficult for her to be comfortable sitting at the table for the duration of a meal.

The digestive problems included intense nausea; Katie threw up as many as seven times a day when we first returned home from the hospital. It was troubling to her and to us. We would stop her feed pump, calculate how much fluid she had lost and try to make up the hydration with sports drinks and feeds, but we did not force her.

It became necessary to request, and learn to use, an intravenous fluid pump at home, in order to rehydrate Katie adequately. Gregg and I were used to maintaining her feeds and her PICC line, but an IV pump was a new piece of machinery. It worked well, and after a few weeks Katie was over the worst of the nausea, and was able to hold her fluids and food. Her IV hydration was ordered through a home-health service, as were the cases of her feeds and heparin (for maintaining her PICC line). Deliveries were coordinated and made to our home.

Katie had to go to the Hem-Onc clinic at the hospital regularly to allow the staff to check her blood, height, weight, and to see how she was recovering. Her follow-on chemo regimen was initiated and monitored. We crushed the Mitotane into applesauce or other soft foods so that she could take it easily (she still could not swallow pills). We also had appointments in the line-care department to have Katie's PICC dressing changed. After a while, her PICC line was removed, as it wasn't being used, and that was a positive and progressive move toward freedom and healing.

One of the happiest follow-up appointments included a stop at Dr. Waldhausen's office, just to say "hello." He proceeded to remove the remaining stitches from Katie's abdomen.

I wanted to find a way to say "thank you" to all of the staff who had been instrumental in Katie's treatment and recovery. Because her case had taken us through many months and several different departments of the hospital, this was a challenge. The idea came to me to contact the **glassybaby** company in Seattle. **Glassybaby** was founded by a cancer survivor, and the company donates some of their proceeds to charity. I asked them if they would make a deal with me, so that I could buy in bulk. They said "yes," so we ordered a variety of colors and picked up about 50 **glassybaby** votives, in gift bags, and took them to the hospital. Katie and I put them in wagons and distributed them throughout the wards to the staff, including in each package a "thank you" card with Katie's photograph. It was rewarding to both of us to see the joyful response from staff when they saw how well Katie looked.

In my family, jewelry is a meaningful gift; my grandparents kept this tradition with us, and my father carried it forward by giving my mother, sister and me gifts of jewelry at significant times in our lives. When Katie was nine years old, my father said that he wanted buy a piece of jewelry for her.

I said, "She is a bit young for that," and he replied, "I know, but I am afraid that I might die before she's old enough for me to do this for her." I encouraged him to go ahead and buy what he wanted to give her, put it in a safe deposit box and wait until she was older. I did not want him to be upset with her if she lost or broke his valuable gift. He assured me that he wouldn't have unrealistic expectations - he just wanted the pleasure of giving it to her. He and my mother went to a jeweler, and selected a beautiful necklace for Katie. She was thrilled and surprised. She enjoyed having such an elegant and grown-up gift, and she wore it on special occasions.

In keeping with this tradition, my mother wanted to give Katie a piece of jewelry in honor of her 12th birthday, and to celebrate the fact that she had come through her treatment and surgery, so she gave Katie a lovely ring. Katie wore both of her rings all of the time after that. At one clinic appointment, I watched as she showed her "bling" to our Childlife and Social Worker, and they shared her happiness. Katie derived great pleasure from wearing these pieces of jewelry, and it made us happy that she was able to enjoy them. She had matured, had survived a great ordeal, and we knew that life is unpredictable – *carpe diem*!

One of our dear friends is an opera singer, who lives in Vienna and sings all over the world; she came to stay in April, which was a big treat for our family. She had visited us before when she was performing in Seattle, but this time, she stayed with us just for fun. That was our first taste of normal family life after Katie's cancer diagnosis - having a houseguest – and it was good.

Katie's wish to have her ears pierced came true once we were back at home. One of our friends, a registered nurse, bought beautiful gold studs and a special piercing instrument, with the necessary sterilizing materials, and she pierced Katie's ears right in our home. She showed Katie how to clean her new earrings and take care of them so that her ears did not become infected. Having that wish come true meant gifts of new earrings, which Katie enjoyed.

The Mitotane caused Katie to experience mild, flu-like symptoms. She started on a low dose and, as her body became accustomed to it, the flu symptoms would abate. Dr. Park would then increase the dose, and the symptoms would resume. Katie had been off of chemotherapy since January, so it seemed a good idea to start maintenance-therapy as soon as possible, to try to kill any remaining cancer cells, and inhibit new ones from growing.

In May, Katie was scheduled to have a PET scan, which is a whole-body image at a molecular level; it's one of the most complete pictures doctors can take of what is happening in the body. We went to the University of Washington's Medical Center for this scan, rather than Children's Hospital, because the PET scanner at Children's was out of commission at that time. We had never been to the U of W hospital before, and it is a very different world than a children's hospital. The U of W is part of the Seattle Cancer Care Alliance, and they work closely with Fred Hutchinson Cancer Research Center and Seattle Children's Hospital, sharing staff and resources, but it has a very different clientele and ambience than Children's.

Katie was not impressed with the décor or the atmosphere, and commented that she was glad that she didn't have to have her cancer treatments at the U of W. This is not to insult that institution, but is an illustration of the importance of specialized, children's hospitals, and how well-suited they are to their clientele. When asked to describe Seattle Children's Hospital briefly, Katie said, *"It's a **hospitable** hospital."*

We were taken to a windowless room where Katie was prepared for the scan. When she was ready, we walked down a hall to the PET room. There was an enormous machine, with a technician's station in an adjacent room - visible through a window. Katie was positioned in the scanner, where it was necessary for her to lie completely motionless; I sat next to her. We were allowed to play music, so we put one of Katie's favorite CDs in a player (the sound track to *Phantom of the Opera),* and let the songs carry us away until the scan was completed. It took a long time; we listened to the entire CD.

The results of the PET scan revealed microscopic bits of tumor in Katie's upper spine and back, and in her liver. The cancer in her back and spine were a surprise, but not the spots in her liver; the pathology reports from the surgery had prepared us for that.

The fact that Katie was taking Mitotane, and that she had had five rounds of chemotherapy, led the doctors to believe that they could monitor her health through her regular clinic visits, and with scans every 3 months. They told us that the chemo would continue working in her body for some time after it was administered, so although we would have much preferred "no evidence of disease," we did not panic at the results of the PET scan.

> *Although we would have much preferred "no evidence of disease," we did not panic at the results of the PET scan*

As soon as she felt well and strong enough, Katie

began to attend the Hutch School with David, commuting via car and ferry with him and Gregg each morning. Katie loved attending the Hutch School; she loved her friends there, and the staff.

Going to this school in Seattle was an experience of independence for Katie and David. Gregg would drop them off at school at 9:00 A.M.; at the end of the school day (1:00 P.M.), they would use their cell phone to call for a taxicab, and would ride in the taxi from school to the ferry dock. While they rode the ferry across the Sound, Katie would take a dose of her medication and they would eat lunch. I would drive to the terminal on our side of the Sound, meet them and take them home. This was a mature and adventurous experience for them to share.

On the days when Katie didn't feel strong or well enough to attend school, Gregg would take David to school on his own, and on those days, David took a Metro bus (rather than a taxicab) from school to the ferry. David grew up a great deal in that time. Before Katie's illness, David had been very reluctant to take public transportation. By May of 2007, he knew which bus to take, where to get on and off of it, and he was able to navigate through downtown Seattle with confidence.

Mother's Day, 2007 was one of my happiest Mother's Days, because Katie had made it safely through her treatment and surgery, and we were back at home together. My family gathered at one of our favorite restaurants - my sister, brother and sister-in-law and parents - and we enjoyed a wonderful meal. Katie was able to taste some of the foods that she hadn't eaten in a long time; it was a great celebration.

Mother's Day, May 2007

This was the beginning of a period in which Katie started to feel good again. She felt less self-conscious as her hair started to grow back; she looked beautiful, and was often compared to a European fashion model. She grew a bit more confident about her appearance; though she still had her NG tube, and it was a nuisance at times, she was accustomed to it. The main annoyance to her was when anyone stared at her – which was ironic, because of Katie's own habit of staring at others.

Gregg's Auntie Bernice was one of our favorite relatives - a strong, warm, outspoken and funny woman. She fell ill at around the same time as Katie did, and we had not been able to see her while we were in Seattle, as she was living in our home town. After we moved back home, we were able to visit Bernice as she was being cared for by the family; by then, she was bedridden. Katie and Auntie Bernice always had a special connection, but there was a something that passed between them during that visit which was beautiful. Somehow, Katie wasn't uncomfortable the way a young person might be around an older person who is ill.

Our precious Auntie Bernice passed away in May. Gregg and I attended her memorial service while the children went to my parents' house for a visit. After the church service, we picked them up and, as is customary in Gregg's family, we took them to a "party" at Bernice's house, hosted by her four sons. Gregg's family is a large, loving Norwegian-American family. Cousins, aunts and uncles were all together eating and visiting, sharing memories. Some of those present had not seen Katie since she went into the hospital, and though it was a sad occasion, we have some wonderful pictures of the cousins together on that day. That was the first big family gathering since Katie had been released from the hospital.

> *Katie asked me, "What if the cancer comes back? What if I die?" I answered her, "If it's humanly possible, we'll get you out of this; we will do everything in our power to save your life."*

Around this time, Katie asked me, "What if the cancer comes back? What if I die?" I answered her honestly and seriously, "If it's humanly possible, we will get you out of this; we will do everything in our power to save your life."

David and Katie were experiencing some changes in their relationship. Though they were having fun together, at times there were conflicts, and this was troubling David. At the Hutch School, the students had mandatory individual counseling, but in addition to that, David asked us to enter family counseling to assist him and Katie. The way David put it was, "Katie and I need to work on our relationship." I admired him very much for bringing this up. Gregg was a reluctant participant, but because David asked for it, we said "Yes."

We found a married couple who were counselors, recommended by a family in our community whose son had survived cancer. We hoped that, with the experiences of their work with the other family, these counselors would have a bit of background in understanding what we were going through. Unfortunately, we did not feel that they comprehended our situation enough to help us.

> *No one knows what it is like, unless they have walked this path, and even then, each family's dynamics and pre-existing conditions are different.*

No one knows what it is like, unless they have walked this path, and still, each family's dynamics and pre-existing conditions are different. It took a great effort to explain things, and even then, the counselors seemed to miss the point, at times. I think the story may have been overwhelming to them, and it was certainly not a common thing to en-counter. How would they know how to offer help?

Katie was struggling with re-entry into her own familiar life, at that time. She was back in the same house with the same people, but all of the puzzle pieces had shifted, and they were not fitting together for her. The counselors split us up, and spoke to us in separate groups of one, two or three. At one point, Katie was in one room with one counselor, while the other was asking questions of the three of us.

Gregg spoke from his heart, and said to the counselor, "If you can help **her** *[Katie]*, you will help all of us. WE are okay; SHE's the one who needs help," which was painful, but true. Gregg wasn't condemning Katie; he was simply saying that most of the emotional dysfunction was occurring within her, at that time.

> *Katie was spinning out of control, because she could not integrate what she had just been through into her old life. It's hard to imagine being 12 years old, and not knowing whether you are going to live or die...her childhood had effectively ended.*

Gregg, David and I had been holding our family together and doing our best to support Katie; now we were back at home, feeling a bit of relief and starting to relax. Katie, however, was spinning out of control, because she could not integrate what she had been through into her old life. It's hard to imagine being 12 years old and not knowing whether you are going to live or die.

Katie had been through an emotional wringer, with poisonous chemicals pumped into her body, a horrific surgery that had left an enormous scar; her body and her privacy had been violated. With all of that, her childhood had effectively ended – and, along with it, the security, freedom and mobility that we assume should belong to us in childhood. I have no idea what that would feel like, but it was clear that some of the time, Katie was practically jumping out of her own skin. Counseling can be useful and helpful in many instances, but these counselors were clearly out of their depth with us, and we knew it. We wanted to support the children in advocating for themselves, and were proud of David for asking for help, but I am not sure that he received help from those sessions; Gregg and I did not.

Vikingfest is a celebration of Norwegian independence which is held annually in our town. Our family has enjoyed the parade, carnival rides, fun fair and food booths, contests, traditional dances, etc. over the years. As the children grew, we allowed them to go to the fair with their friends, and this year, Katie wanted very much to do that. She could finally fit into her favorite clothes again, after spending months wearing pajamas and hospital gowns, during chemo, surgery and recovery. She wanted to put on her cutest clothes and go downtown to mingle with her friends. Even with an NG-tube and very short hair, this was her first social opportunity in town, and Katie was not going to miss it. Katie met her best friend and they went downtown together, while David joined his friends. People were very glad to see Katie, and though some stared and were openly curious about her appearance, she was glad to participate in *Vikingfest* again.

Our wedding anniversary is in May, so Gregg and I hoped to be able to go away for a quick overnight trip. My parents offered to take care of the children and manage all of Katie's healthcare needs, so, although it was nerve-wracking to leave them together, we did. We desperately needed a break. Gregg drove us to the ferry and we rode it to Victoria, B.C.

After just a few hours away, we received a phone call from home, saying that Katie was experiencing back pain, and they couldn't find her pain medication. We hadn't sent pain medication with her, so I told them where to find it at home, and reminded them to check the dosage carefully. Katie told us, "I wish you were here; I don't want them to take care of this," but my parents assured us that they would be fine, and told us not to worry. With some ambivalence, we stayed where we were, and celebrated our anniversary. It wasn't restful, because I could not help but worry about Katie, but I tried to give my attention to enjoying our little "escape."

When we got home, everyone was fine, but we noticed that Katie's NG tube was not in its normal place. It was not clear how it had been moved, but once we realized it was out of place, we moved it back where it belonged without difficulty. That was a moment when we realized how far we had come. The simplest things could go wrong, and although we knew how to deal with them, the rest of the family (and most of the world) did not. That was a minor issue, however, and we deeply appreciated my parents' awareness of the fact that we needed respite care, and their willingness to step in and provide it.

Katie and David had been invited to apply to the American Cancer Society's Camp Goodtimes West for a week during the summer. It is a camp for children who have cancer (and their siblings), and our dear friend, Paul has been involved with this camp for over 20 years. Katie's oncologist said there was no medical reason for Katie not to go – in fact, Dr. Park was supportive of the idea. Some of the nurses who had taken care of Katie in the hospital were also going to be on staff at camp.

I had always wanted the children to experience summer camp, and we felt that this week would be a good time for Katie to reintegrate further into normal teenage living, and that it would help her get ready to go back to school in the fall. We hoped that the children would have fun, make friends and enjoy new experiences, but Katie did *not* want to go.

Gregg and I made an "executive decision" to send them to camp in spite of Katie's reluctance, and fortunately, David was easy-going, but Katie initiated a lot of arguments about it.

One night, Katie claimed that she was going to kill herself; she grabbed a pair of scissors and tried to cut herself. We were horrified; we took the scissors away from her and let her know that this behavior was not an acceptable way to deal with her frustrations. Katie was distraught and hard to understand; she said that she didn't want to live anymore, and at that point, I became deeply worried.

I have had some training in lay ministry, and have been taught what to do in case of suicide threats. Because of this, I felt that we should take Katie to the hospital; no suicide threat should ever be taken lightly. Gregg disagreed with me; he felt that Katie was not serious, but was trying to manipulate us, so we were in complete disagreement as to how to deal with this problem, which was emergent,

> *We were in complete disagreement as to how to deal with this problem, which was emergent, right in front of us, & needed resolution immediately.*

right in front of us, and needed resolution immediately. Unfortunately, David was present - and a witness to all of the chaos.

It was simply surreal and unthinkable. To have Katie say that she wanted to die was particularly hard to fathom, since we had just spent the past seven months trying desperately to save her life! We had never encountered a suicide threat in our lives; I knew that we were out of our depth. Drawing from what I had been taught, I knew that the first thing to do is to **get help**, and I knew that Gregg and I were not going to be able to *be* "help," in this scenario.

I felt that we should bundle Katie up, pack an overnight bag and take her directly to Children's Hospital; Gregg felt that that was a complete overreaction. He said that if I decided to take Katie to the hospital, I would have to go alone with her. At this point, Katie was nearly my height, and out of control emotionally, so it was simply not possible for me to take her on my own. I could have called 911, but it did not occur to me at the time.

> *This was a moment of utter family breakdown; it was one of the lowest points on our journey. The emotional chaos which Katie was displaying was one of the many side effects of her cancer diagnosis and treatment.*

This was a moment of utter family breakdown; it was one of the lowest points on our journey. The emotional chaos which Katie was displaying was one of the many side effects of her cancer diagnosis and treatment.

As we were trying to come to agreement on what to do, Katie relented and said, "I was not serious; I won't really kill myself." At that point, part of my mind said, "Gregg was right;" but I also knew that Katie could have been saying this simply to avoid going to the hospital for evaluation. I told her very seriously, "Don't you ever use that threat again; don't you EVER pretend about suicide, because I will take you in! I can't help you with that; that's out of my bailiwick - way out of my league." Katie elaborated, and told us why she was angry: for the simple reason that we had made her come downstairs at a time when she didn't want to do so. That is one of the most searing memories I have, in the wake of all of the fallout from cancer – her total loss of perspective and threat to harm herself.

She was falling apart inside, and the counseling was not adequate to help her; we couldn't fully relieve her, either. She did threaten suicide again, but she didn't act on it - she recanted again, and never tried to harm herself. It was a hair-raising and terrifying experience, and was very hard on David, as well as on our marriage. It takes time to come back to balance, after going through such stark, terrifying emotional landscapes.

Katie's need of everything I had to give showed me a strength I didn't know I possessed. She gave me the gift of coming into my own, in the fullest sense, but at a great price to her, and to all of us. In fact, there were many changes in me throughout this journey. One thing that changed was my outlook on marriage. I finally understood why people embark upon affairs, and I began to view that behavior with more compassion.

Earlier in my life, I believed that if my spouse was unfaithful to me, I would divorce him immediately. That feeling changed when we were living in Ronald McDonald House; I understood why people cheat, why they gamble, why they drink too much, or overeat - I got it. It wasn't personal; it wasn't about anything lacking in one's partner – it was like a pressure-relief valve. Once I understood that, I began to believe that I could forgive anything, especially in those circumstances.

Our disagreement as to how to deal with Katie's suicide threats was very distressing to me, and I was miserable about Gregg's response and the way it had played out between us, but I learned as events unfolded further that one has to give time to one's partner; one has to make countless allowances in a marriage, if one wants the marriage to endure.

It takes great amounts of love, patience and compassion for a marriage to survive extreme situations like those that we experienced. Katie's illness has changed the way I've approached our marriage. We are in this together; no one shares these particular memories except Gregg, David and me, so we have a unique understanding of one another. We are also uniquely wounded by what we've been through.

> *It takes great amounts of love, patience and compassion for a marriage to survive such extreme situations.*

In June of 2007, the school year ended. David finished ninth grade and Katie completed sixth grade. That left us free for the summer! We went to Katie's and David's public schools to register for the autumn term.

Katie decided not to go back to her private school, so I took her to enroll in the local public junior high, and David to the high school. That was exciting, but a bit worrying, because Katie was still weak when we went through the registration process.

We realized that the school was going to need to create a special plan for her. She was a little bit behind her class, academically. She would need to go to the nurse's office to take her medication during the day; that was a new issue. An even bigger problem was working out how Katie was going to get around the campus between her classes, carrying a backpack.

Katie & David enjoying a water fight at home,
May, 2007

It was encouraging to see Katie and David playing
outside again. Though she was still frail, the two of
them had squirt-gun fights and rode the rope swing
in our woods. They made videos and played with
Playmobil. Every single thing that they resumed of
their "old life" brought joy and hope to me.

Katie began to invite friends over. That indicated
great progress, because she had been so anti-social in

the hospital. She allowed me to enroll her in the community theatre program which she had so enjoyed the previous summer; David chose to take tennis lessons instead, in preparation for high school tennis team tryouts in the autumn.

I drove Katie to her theatre camp, but after the first few sessions, she began to complain of back pain and fatigue. One day, when I arrived to pick her up, I found her resting on a couch in the theatre's office. I wasn't sure if she was being contrary and not trying to participate, or if she really wasn't feeling well enough. I let her decide what to do, and she chose to drop out of the program. That raised my concern, but I didn't want to push her too much. She had to recover at her own pace.

We celebrated Father's Day at my parents' house. Katie was feeling pretty well, and we took funny videos of that gathering with my side of the family. Near the end of June, David and Katie went to Camp Goodtimes West for six days. Everyone who attends camp has cancer, or has had cancer, or has a sibling who has had cancer. Katie's NG tube was not remarkable at camp, surgical scars were not exceptional and baldness did not matter; camp was a totally accepting place where everyone understands the pediatric cancer journey. Both David and Katie had a happy time that week. Though Katie did not want to go, right up to the moment we left her and David at camp, later on we found out that she had loved it.

The week that the children spent at camp was a time for Gregg and me to regroup, refresh, rest and be on our own. That was hugely helpful to us, after the previous, exhausting eight months; it was a great gift to know that both of the children were in capable hands, with well-trained counselors, nurses and an oncologist on staff at all times. I relaxed a bit, for the first time since Katie was admitted to the hospital on October 10th. It's hard to adequately express the value that week had for all of us.

Katie dancing at Camp Goodtimes West, June 2007

When we picked up the children from camp during the first week of July, Katie had a crazy hairdo leftover from the camp carnival; she did not want to wash it out, so she wore a rainbow-colored hairdo in a Mohawk style, with glitter in it, for several days afterward. She had been featured on the front page of the local newspaper in an article about camp, and was happy about that.

We went straight from camp to a family gathering, where Katie was invited to be a bridesmaid in her cousin's wedding in February, 2008. Katie was thrilled, because one of her life's dreams was to be a bridesmaid, and it was finally going to happen! We were excited to hear that our niece and her boyfriend, both of whom we love, had decided to get married.

Once back at home, Katie told us that she had experienced fatigue and back-pain at camp; at first, we thought that was natural, due to the increased activity of the camp program, and the fact that a camp bed was less comfortable than her bed at home, but it continued, and grew worse in July. She had some stiffness, which I thought could be due to the scar tissue from her surgery, because so many of her muscles had been cut. We engaged both massage therapy and physical therapy to increase her flexibility and comfort, and to help strengthen her core. Physical therapy included a bit of mat work, as well as exercises in a swimming pool to help her relax and stretch, easily and gently. She wasn't happy about having physical therapy, but we would take a soak in the hot tub afterwards, and she loved that. Our massage therapist gently worked on Katie's scar tissue, which made her feel much better; in fact, both Katie and David enjoyed and benefited from massage therapy.

While we sat in the hot tub after physical therapy, we began to think ahead to Thanksgiving vacation, when we would go to Palm Desert again for David's birthday and my mom's birthday, so we made airline reservations for our trip in November. It was especially exciting that year, because we had had to cancel in 2006; planning the trip for 2007 signified a return to our normal family traditions and activities.

> *I was happy to have an opportunity to thank the hospital for all they had done for us, and to help them to raise money and awareness.*

We were invited to speak at a Children's Hospital fundraiser hosted by the Steve Pool-Warren Moon Guild in the middle of July. I was happy to say "yes" to this invitation, because it gave us an opportunity to thank the hospital for all they had done for us, and to help them to raise money and awareness. The guild is a prominent one, with many professional athletes and broadcasters supporting it.

It was an exciting event for our family; I was to speak, and all four of us would be on stage together, dressed in our best, for the paddle-raising, when people pledge money, rather than (or in addition to) buying something during the auction.

I wrote and practiced delivering my speech, and when the day arrived, we drove onto the ferry. Unfortunately, Katie got sick on the way over to the event. She was nauseous, uncomfortable and clearly would have been miserable spending hours at a benefit, so we reluctantly called my brother and sister-in-law, and asked them to meet us on the other side of the water. They took Katie to their house to rest. I felt terribly torn, because I hated to leave her when she was sick, but I also felt that I couldn't cancel at the last minute, when the guild was counting on me to be their speaker.

I gave my talk about all that the hospital had done for our family, and then the audience was asked to "raise your paddles" for different levels of support. Gregg, David and I stood on stage and watched in amazement as nearly $110,000 was pledged in just a few minutes! I wished that Katie could have seen it happening, all because of her story. People were very kind and complimentary about the speech, which encouraged me, because I had been very nervous. I was happy to be able to help the guild, but was also preoccupied and concerned about Katie. As soon as we could politely do so, we left to get Katie and take her home.

Katie's pain and weakness continued and increased. I called our pediatrician and requested a scan for Katie, because her life was getting harder, instead of improving. While the pediatrician examined her and ordered an x-ray, Katie had a severe attack of pain. I gave her pain medication, waited for it to take

> *I told Gregg, "I have a bad feeling about this; you need to skip work tomorrow and come with us."*

effect, and took her for the x-ray. After reading the results, the pediatrician told us that we needed to go to Seattle Children's Hospital for a CT scan.

I told Gregg, "I have a bad feeling about this; you need to skip work tomorrow and come with us." He took the day off, and we went over to the hospital with Katie; we were scheduled for one of the first appointments of the day. That meant going in early enough so that Katie could take the contrast dye into her NG tube, and then waiting until it was well into her system and visible for the scan. After she finished taking in the dye, we were taken to wait in one of the windowless, private rooms near the CT room.

We had given Katie some medication (Ativan) to help her to be calm and to prevent nausea that morning, and when we got into the private room, she began to hallucinate, pointing to the clock on the wall and saying, "Why are the numbers melting?" That was a bit alarming; she had not hallucinated since being in the CICU after her surgery. There was nothing to do but comfort her and wait; we waited for a long time, and no one came to take us in for the CT scan. This was not normal.

After a while, we heard doctors' names being called on the paging system - cardiac doctors who we knew from the CICU. Then we heard rapid footsteps in the hall, outside of the door, and after a while, a staff member came in and told us, "The child who had the CT scan before your appointment has coded, and they are working on him now. You will have to wait until they can stabilize him and sterilize the room, which will take a while." I felt deep concern for that family, and began to pray for them and their child.

We waited in that windowless room for three hours; Gregg and I both got hungry, and took turns going to the cafeteria to eat. There was no question of moving Katie. Eventually, someone came and took us into the CT room. We put on lead aprons, as usual, so that we could stay with Katie during her scan; by this time, she was a little more aware.

The radiologist who reviewed Katie's pictures was not one of the staff who we were accustomed to seeing; Dr. Park had specially requested him to come in to read Katie's scans. He greeted us afterward, and was very solicitous - he offered us beverages, vouchers for the cafeteria and a wheelchair for Katie. I thought that was a bit odd, because it had never happened before. He said that Dr. Park wanted to see us up in the clinic, and that she would go over the results of the scan with us.

We went up to the Hematology-Oncology clinic, got settled into an exam room with Katie lying on the table. Katie's oncologist came in to the exam room to talk with us. She is a fairly serious person, and on that day, she came in looking very serious indeed. She closed the door to the exam room behind her, stood by it and said, "Katie, I promised that I would never lie to you. I don't have good news for you today; your cancer is back." We were undone by that announcement.

> *The doctor said, "Katie, I promised that I would never lie to you. I don't have good news for you today; your cancer is back."*

I'm sure that, in the back of my mind, I knew things were not going well – Katie's increasing pain and weakness were not good signs - but she was taking the maintenance drug, Mitotane, and she had survived that huge surgery. Katie had had a PET scan just a couple of months before, and the few remaining tumor cells were microscopic, at that point. The doctors had told us repeatedly that this was a slow-growing cancer. It was mind-boggling to learn that it had returned so quickly. Dr. Park told us that a new tumor had grown, as large as the original tumor, in the weeks since Katie's scan in May.

Katie then said the bravest thing I had ever heard her say, which was "Then I'll have surgery." Surgery had been her greatest fear before being admitted to the hospital, and having survived the arduous, 18-hour ordeal (and six weeks of tough recovery afterwards in the hospital, not to mention many more weeks of weakness and illness at home) - for her to volunteer to have another surgery was a most courageous decision. It was therefore all the more awful to hear the doctor tell her "I'm sorry, but it's not in a place where we can remove it by surgery."

Dr. Park gave us a little time to adjust to that news, and then our Childlife and Social Workers came to be with Katie, so that Dr. Park and the nurses could talk to Gregg and me privately. I remember holding Katie in my arms and hearing her ask, "How could this happen?" The same question was going through my mind.

We asked Katie's permission to leave her with Julie and Tanya for a few minutes, so that we could go to another room to speak with Dr. Park, and she said "Yes." Gregg and I walked down the hall, sat down in a small consulting room, and asked Dr. Park and the nurse what was going to happen to Katie. They told us that the cancer was in her spinal column and her bones, and that she was probably going to become paralyzed.

We asked if they had any idea how long she would live, and they said, "If we guess, we are always wrong, so we don't guess." We asked them what we could do for her, how to keep her comfortable and so on. "What can you give us? How will we take care of her? What do you do for a child who is dying?" We had no idea. We had never been responsible for a dying person's care. To care for a dying child – our child – sounded like a frightening responsibility.

They told us that they would prescribe drugs to help us keep Katie comfortable, and that they would continue to give us help and support. They also offered to call hospice for us, and we quickly accepted that offer. They called our county's hospice, and coincidentally, one of our neighbors (who works for hospice) answered the telephone. How awful for our kind neighbor, to learn that Katie was going to die as she answered the phone at her office.

Dr. Park offered us the option to take Katie in for radiation therapy, and we asked how that would benefit her. Dr. Park said that it might slow the growth of the tumor. We asked if it would save her life, and she said "No, but it might prolong it." I asked where this was available, and was told that Katie would have to go to the University of Washington hospital for radiation. That helped us to decide against the idea of taking Katie, who was already feeling weak and ill, on a ferry trip and car ride for over an hour, to a hospital that she didn't like, to take treatment that would not cure her cancer.

On top of the travel involved, considering the side effects of radiation, it just didn't seem to us to be *kind* to do that to Katie. We felt that radiation treatment would ruin her quality and enjoyment of life, so we declined that option. We learned in that meeting with Dr. Park that some parents will do *anything* to prolong their child's life, but we did not feel that way. We wanted to give Katie the best quality of life she could possibly have, for the time she had left – however long that was - and we did not want her to experience any more suffering.

> *We learned that some parents will do anything to prolong their child's life, but we did not feel that way. We wanted to give Katie the best quality of life she could possibly have – and we did not want her to experience any more suffering.*

I don't remember much more of that conversation. After it ended, we rejoined Katie in the exam room. The oncology staff ordered all of the medications that we needed for Katie from the hospital's in-house pharmacy. We were told that we could pick them up before we left to catch the ferry for home.

Gregg took Katie to the car while I waited at the pharmacy. I made phone calls while I waited. David was at home, since when we had left in the morning, we had thought, again, that we were simply going to the hospital for a scan. I called my parents, gave them the terrible news, and asked them to bring dinner to David at our house, and to wait with him until we arrived at home.

> *As I tried my best to maintain a polite demeanor, my mind was screaming, "I'm trying to go home – we were just told that our daughter is going to die - could I please just have her drugs NOW?"*

I expected that the pharmacy would expedite this order, because I assumed that, from reading the contents, they would know that we had just received the worst news of our life. Our daughter was dying, and we wanted to take her home as quickly as possible. I went to the pharmacy window, asked for our order, and found that it was not ready, so I resigned myself to waiting.

I made more telephone calls to our family and members of our closest support system. Upon returning to the pharmacy window, I found that the prescriptions were still not ready. As I tried my best to maintain a polite demeanor and behavior, my mind was screaming: *I'm trying to go home – we live over an hour away – we were just told that our daughter is going to die - could I please just have the drugs NOW!*

One of the medications prescribed for Katie was methadone, which is a controlled substance, and they could not release a controlled substance instantly. I suppose that there is a process that they are required to go through, but I will always remember how draining, frustrating and sad that waiting period was for me. They were professional and kind but it seemed to take an agonizingly long time, under the circumstances.

When I finally got back to the car, we drove to the ferry dock and onto the boat. Katie seemed to be dazed, as she had been on and off all day long. I asked her if she wanted me to sit in the back seat with her, but she said "No." She stretched out with her blanket, while Gregg and I sat in the front seats.

About halfway through the boat ride, Katie raised her voice and cried, "I'm going to die! I'm going to die!" to which Gregg replied, very quietly, "Yes, you are." That is when I burst into tears. I'll never forget that trip. I asked Katie, "Please, can I come back and sit with you now?" and she said, "Yes." I climbed in the back seat with her and held her in my arms.

When we arrived at home, David was there with my parents, and we had to tell him the awful news that his sister was going to die.

That was the third time we had been told that Katie was going to die. We had heard it when we first got to the hospital in October of 2006, and later, in the middle of Katie's surgery on February 21, 2007; but now, in the summer of 2007, she really *was* going to die. Having heard it twice before made it less shocking than having no warning, but it was still unbelievably devastating news. We were all stunned, and terribly sad.

Later that evening, a friend came over and reviewed the medications with us, helping us to organize a schedule to keep ahead of Katie's pain. There were many new, unfamiliar drugs to dispense; because of the effects of shock, it was very helpful to have our friend, who worked in the medical field, with us to work out a straightforward approach to the new medication routine. Once we had a schedule in place, I felt calmer about being able to handle whatever was to come.

We sent out an online message to everyone we knew, because I could not face making dozens of phone calls, saying over and over again, "We've had some bad news, and you need to know that Katie is going to die." I just couldn't do it, except to the immediate circle of family and closest friends, so I put the message on Katie's caringbridge site as an update. Soon, beautiful messages of support began to arrive in response to the terrible news.

Chapter 7:

Somewhere, Over the Rainbow

I felt that our job now was to make everything as easy as possible for Katie. She had been through so much hardship, and had done everything that was required of her. Now that we knew that a cure was impossible, we needed to give her every tool to ease her way. I've heard that there are parents who won't let go - who try to get their children to hold on, to "fight" their disease and live as long as possible for the *parents'* sake. I cannot imagine putting that kind of pressure on a dying child. I wanted Katie to be free, to know that she was loved every step of the way, to be peaceful and at ease.

The CT scan took place on July 20th, 2007. A few days later, a hospice social worker and nurse came to our home, to meet Katie and discuss the situation with us. They were wonderful women; they reviewed certain medications that hadn't been explained to us at the hospital, and told us how they could support Katie and us.

The nurse, Amy, put a few new medicines into our refrigerator. I asked her what they were and what was their purpose (these were not on the daily medication list). About one of them, Amy answered calmly, "This is to help with secretions, though we may not need it." I wondered, "Secretions…what is Katie going to *secrete*?" I didn't know what that meant, in the context of dying, but I didn't want to find out.

Medication schedule during Hospice care

The medication schedule became very complex at this time. Some medications were needed once a day; some were given two, and others three times per day. I entered everything necessary into a computer program, and coded each medication with a different color, so that there would be no errors or omissions. I printed each week's schedule ahead of time, and made notes as to what was happening, so that I could report each change or question to Amy during her visits or phone calls.

Amy came to check on Katie every few days. That was reassuring to me, since I didn't know how to take care of someone who was going to die, much less my own child. Amy became a lifeline for me, with her kind, calm demeanor – she is sweet, funny and a faithful person.

Amy did her work as unobtrusively as possible. I bonded with her right away; she reminded me of our beloved pediatrician, Diane, who had died in 2005. There was something about Amy's presence that was deeply comforting to me. However, Katie did not see Amy that way; perhaps it was because she knew that hospice had come to help because she was dying.

One day Katie expressed her distress about having to accept Amy's help: "She's here to help me die!" I replied, "No, she is here to help make your life more comfortable."

Because we've watched British TV, Katie began referring to Amy as "the quack," which is a disparaging British term for a doctor. Instead of talking about Amy by name, Katie would ask me, "Is *the quack* still here?" She never did this in front of Amy, but I told her about it; Amy thought it was hilarious.

During her visits to check on Katie, Amy was always tender and respectful. She asked Katie for permission to examine her on each visit, and would then listen to her heart, take her blood pressure and so on. Amy did not ask Katie embarrassing questions; she understood her age and condition. It was clear to me that she cared deeply for Katie. Amy later wrote a beautiful book called "The Lamaze of Dying," and Katie is one of the people to whom she dedicated it.

> *Katie took to calling Amy "the quack," and said, "She's here to help me die!" to which I replied, "No, she is here to make your life more comfortable."*

In the beginning of hospice care, Katie was strong enough to walk around the house and go up and downstairs. She watched movies and visited with close friends and family who came to spend time with her. She would go outside on our deck and play with the cats. She did not discuss her diagnosis with those who came to visit.

Andrea, our niece – the one who had invited Katie to be a bridesmaid in her wedding to Mike - asked us if they should move their wedding to an earlier date. We said, "We don't want to tell you when to get married - but it might be a good idea." They asked "How soon?" and we answered that we didn't know, but sooner would be better, because we had been told that Katie was likely to become paralyzed.

The result of this discussion was that Mike and Andrea planned and executed their wedding in 10 days. One of Mike's brothers was living in Switzerland; their father called him and said, "It's time to come home," so he flew back from Switzerland to be present for the wedding.

Bridesmaid Katie & Groomsman (cousin) Joey walking down the aisle, August 2, 2007

Everyone in the family came together: family members organized the food and wine, our friend Paul took hundreds of beautiful photographs; and the wedding took place at the bride's family home on a perfectly sunny day - August 2nd, 2007. Katie was not strong enough to go shopping with the wedding party, so she participated in the selection of the bridesmaid dresses online. I ordered gorgeous satin sandals to match her dress. Katie appreciated beautiful clothes, and she loved the fact that she was able to wear a real bridesmaid's dress and do her part as Andrea's maid of honor. This event took place two weeks after we found out that Katie was terminally ill.

Andrea & Mike's Wedding party, August 2, 2007

We treasure the photographs of that wedding day. Katie didn't participate in any of the festivities, except for the ceremony, because she was too frail. She chose to spend most of the day resting upstairs in the master bedroom, not downstairs in the midst of the activity, where she would have had to socialize. People came upstairs to visit her, and the rest of the time, she watched videos on her iPod. I brought a cooler with all of her medications for the day; she needed a number of doses of morphine to get through it all, because standing and walking were becoming increasingly difficult for her.

When we came home after the wedding and reception, I asked Katie, "How was it for you to be a bridesmaid? Was it as good as you dreamed it would be?" and she said yes, it was. I consider that wedding day to be Katie's "Make-A-Wish," because that was one of her dreams in life: to be a bridesmaid.

> *When Katie was dying, we experienced similar emotional issues to those at the beginning of her illness: shock, disbelief, sadness.*

When Katie was dying, we experienced similar emotional issues to those at the beginning of her illness: shock, disbelief, sadness. Once again, it was hard to hear Katie talking about her own death; I could hardly bear to face it. We were still being cared for and supported by Seattle Children's Hospital staff, even though we were at home. Our Childlife worker reminded me, tenderly and respectfully, in effect: "You're up; you have to do this." I realized, again, that this was part of my job as Katie's mother.

Bath time was still a very private "mom and me" time. Katie continued to like to have me read *Nancy Drew* mysteries to her while she was in the bathtub.

She also began to reveal her grief to me, speaking of how she felt about her own death, her life's dreams and her sadness over the things that she was going to miss. She spoke of her regrets and her losses. This was very hard to bear, but I bore it as best I could. Open-hearted listening was a precious gift that I could give to Katie. There was so little I could do to "make it better," but listening was something that could help to ease her pain. So I listened, and I grieved with her.

> *She began to tell me how she felt about her own death, her life's dreams and her sadness over the things that she was going to miss. This was very hard to bear, but listening was something I could do to help ease her pain.*

Eventually, Katie gave us some instructions about her memorial service ("I want a party, like Auntie Bernice's, and I want fireworks"), and she asked us to scatter her ashes at Camp Goodtimes West. In light of her abject refusal to go to camp, the episodes of fighting about it, and all of the emotional drama that surrounded the camp decision, we were very surprised at this request. The fact that she asked us to scatter her ashes there told us, without a doubt, how positive her camp experience had been. We knew that we had been right to push her, even beyond her comfort level, on that particular decision.

I asked Katie's permission to scatter some of her ashes in the Sound at the family home (where my parents live), because I want my ashes scattered there, too. She gave me permission to do that.

Katie wrote a will. No one told her to do this; she thought of it herself. She wrote her will in longhand, on notebook paper. She left her shoes to me, because we share a passion for shoes; she left her Playmobil to David; she left half of her bank account to the Goodwill charitable organization, and the other half to be split equally between David, Gregg, and me. She left the window seat in her bedroom to me, her clothes and toys to any charity we chose, and her books to the library.

It was astonishing to me, that a 12-year-old would have the courage and presence of mind to make a will. In a situation in which many of us would feel sorry for ourselves and powerless, to take whatever power she could find, to use it for good and make her mark with it…I admire her very much for that positive action. Her will is a treasure, to me.

You may recall that when a palliative care team member came to Katie's room early in her cancer journey, I was resentful and a bit angry with him for introducing his services when we felt we did not need them. I told our support system, "We will call if we need palliative care" – and now, with a terminal diagnosis, we recognized that we desperately needed hospice. I welcomed their presence. Dee, our hospice Social Worker, helped David as much as she could, and was gentle, supportive and caring toward all of us.

When Amy came to check on Katie, I would go for a run or a walk for about half an hour. This time of exercise also allowed me to let off steam, to cry, pray and listen to music in privacy. Eva Cassidy's version of "Over the Rainbow" used to play in my head, and I would grieve for all that Katie was losing – all of the dreams that would never come true for her in this world. I would often pray for mercy for Katie as I ran in the summer sun.

> *The thought of a child going on without her parents, her family, is a gut-wrenching one to a mother, whose every instinct from conception is to keep her child safe – to love, tend, comfort and provide for her child's needs. Everything in me screamed that Katie needed her family with her*

It is against nature for a child to die before her parents. It was painful to think of my daughter going away from me, on her own, to a place I could not prepare for her. I tried to think of it as if she was going away to college – I told myself that she would be alive in some way, somewhere, but in a place we couldn't visit – a place from which she couldn't return. I never got very far with this imagery, but I tried to use it to help prepare myself to let her go. She was only 12 and a half – too young to travel to an unknown place without us!

The thought of a child going on without her parents, her family, is a gut-wrenching one to a mother, whose every instinct from conception is to keep her child safe – to love, tend, comfort and provide for her child's needs. Everything in me screamed that Katie needed her family with her, but we didn't have any control over the fact that we could not accompany her where she was going. We had to adjust, and quickly, in order to support her in her adjustment. I had to do my best to be with her through whatever came, and not to communicate resistance or fear, but instead love, peace, patience and comfort. This was some of the hardest work I've ever been called to do.

After the wedding, going up and down stairs became too difficult for her, so Katie stayed in her bedroom. I asked her if she wanted us to set up a bed for her downstairs so that she could be with us in the midst of all of the daily family activity, and she looked at me as if to ask, "Are you out of your mind?" It was clear that she wanted to be in her own room, with as much privacy as possible. We bought a baby monitor so that she could call us if she needed anything, yet still have her room to herself.

Pain became an issue when we were initially getting accustomed to Katie's new diagnosis and the regimen of medications. No one knew quite how the disease was going to progress, as it is such a rare cancer, but it had certainly proved that it was aggressive, growing rapidly between May and July.

In the beginning, it was difficult to anticipate how her pain was going to manifest. Katie was taking methadone as an underlying pain-management agent, and had morphine for breakthrough pain, with other medications for nerve pain and inflammation. We had stopped the Mitotane (oral chemo), because it obviously wasn't working. At Amy's suggestion, we reduced the quantity of Katie's feeds, because she wasn't up and about, burning many calories.

Katie had a couple of horrible breakthrough-pain episodes, when the pain got ahead of her medication, and we learned very quickly from those. One of the most important things that Katie learned at this time - and another admirable achievement on her part – was to listen to her body. She found that, just before the surges of pain occurred, she experienced an "aura" that predicted them. She learned to identify a feeling in her body, which arose before the pain escalated, broke through the medications and became so intense that she couldn't endure it. She had two severe episodes that caused her to cry out in pain, before she learned to identify this aura. At one point, she screamed, "I want to die NOW! I want to die *now*." That is a searing, traumatic memory, for me.

> *Katie found that, just before a surge of pain occurred, she experienced an "aura" that predicted it. She had two severe episodes that caused her to cry out in pain, before she learned to identify this aura. At one point, she screamed, "I want to die NOW!" That is a searing, traumatic memory.*

What we learned to do when the pain began to escalate was to give Katie a bolus of morphine immediately, through her NG tube, and wait 20 minutes to see if that was enough. If one bolus didn't give her relief, we gave her a second dose of morphine. If *that* wasn't enough to alleviate the pain, in 20 more minutes we would give her a third bolus, and then call Amy to tell her that the pain was escalating. Amy would then direct us to increase the underlying dose of methadone a certain amount, in order to address this.

When the pain was intense, while we waited for the morphine to take effect, I would try to comfort Katie in some way. I would massage her, if she wanted that, or lie down with her, gently telling her it was going to pass, or just be with her, quietly. Once we learned how to manage it – after those two episodes - the pain never again got out of control. I'm thankful for that.

If a patient is on heavy pain medication, it slows down her digestive system, and that can contribute to pain. Amy warned us that this could become a problem, and it did. We tried to resolve it with home remedies recommended by Amy (prune juice and 7-up, senna, etc.) but they were not adequate, so Amy came over to manually clear Katie's colon. This was something that I felt sure that Katie would not want to endure, but it was necessary.

For this procedure, Katie was medicated to keep her drowsy and comfortable. We put one of her favorite movies in the DVD player, and at Amy's recommendation, Katie and I lay on the bed facing one another, with my arms around her. Katie had her back to Amy, and while Amy worked silently, the movie played in the background. By this time, Katie knew a lot of movies by heart, so she was mouthing the words to the movie and focusing on the dialogue, while I was holding her in my arms.

It is hard to fathom the violation of a young girl's privacy and her personal space caused by this procedure; it was necessary for her health and well-being, and Katie knew this, but it was still unpleasant and invasive.

Amy did the job professionally and unobtrusively, and when she had finished, Katie looked over her shoulder at Amy and asked, "Do you really like looking up people's buttholes?" It was a classic "Katie" remark – the way that she dealt with the situation and tossed off that kind of quip was Katie's way of cutting the whole thing down to size. Under normal circumstances, I would not have allowed my children to talk to anyone in that way, but these were not normal circumstances, and I admired her for putting the entire thing in perspective, in her own unique way.

> *Katie looked at Amy and asked, "Do you like looking up people's buttholes?" A classic "Katie" remark – the way that she tossed off that kind of quip was Katie's way of cutting the whole thing down to size.*

After Katie learned to recognize the aura that would precede a breakthrough pain episode, we kept a pre-loaded syringe of morphine by her bedside so that she could connect it to her NG-tube and give herself a dose when needed. We gave her a notebook with a pen to keep by her bedside, and when Katie gave herself a bolus of morphine, she would write the time in the notebook. I went in and out of her room often during the day, to take care of her medication and hydration needs, so Katie liked taking care of this herself. After Katie gave herself a dose of morphine, I reloaded the syringe for the next time she needed it. This arrangement afforded Katie a measure of autonomy, control, and privacy.

Every so often, she would request gummy worms, licorice, pretzels or other foods that she had not wanted to eat in many months, and it was good to see her enjoying food again, even if it was snack food. When she was drowsy, she would fall asleep with a gummy worm or pretzels hanging out of her mouth, and I remember thinking "That's dangerous – she could choke!" and then, realizing how absurd that thought was, because Katie was dying. It was hard to take in that fact - my protective "mother instinct" was still operating at full strength, worrying about her choking.

Katie found the memory of Diane (her pediatrician, who had died of breast cancer) to be a comfort and inspiration; she told me during this period that Diane had come to visit her. I was a bit surprised to hear this, but calmly asked her what Diane had said. "She told me not to be afraid, but to watch out for the first step," Katie replied. That sounded like a line from a movie, but I didn't doubt her. A week or so later, when I asked her if Diane had been back to talk again, Katie said to me, in withering tones, "No, Mom, I'm only talking to *living* people these days." I knew to let it go at that – and not to ask again.

Childlife had advised me not to hide my feelings from Katie - that she would know that I was being false if I held my emotions in too tightly - but I am the kind of mother who does not want to burden my children with my troubles. "The buck stops here" - I want my children to know that they are safe with me, and that they can say whatever they need to say to me; I want them to know that I can handle it. That is how I see my job. However, one day, Katie and I were watching one of her movies, one which involved a family whose mother had died. The father was doing his best to bring up the children on his own, but the girls were getting out of hand, and when the movie ended, I began to cry.

I said to Katie, "I feel terrible, because I wanted to give you so much, but we ran out of time. I was planning to give you everything in its time, but I didn't want to spoil you, like those girls in the movie." Katie said to me, "You're the best mom a girl ever had." I replied "No, I'm not. I do a lot of things wrong."

> *Katie said to me, "Mom, you have got to stop apologizing."*

That is when Katie said to me something which I will always remember: *"Mom, you have got to stop apologizing."*

I told Katie, "I'm going to miss you every day; I will think about you every day, and send love to you every day, and when I die, I'll come looking for you." She replied, "You won't have to look for me; I'll be waiting for you." Then she made a motion as if to take a handful of her heart, and she put it on my heart and said, "Now I'll always be in here." I did the same thing for her, and cried, and we held each other. I told her not to worry about me, but to go whenever she needed to go. I told her that I would walk every step of the way with her, "until the door slams in my face," - until I was not allowed to go any farther.

Katie tried to be as independent as she could through all of this, but as she grew weaker, even walking to the bathroom to use the toilet became too difficult, because she was unable to stand up, unaided, from a sitting position. She would call for me, and it would take all of my strength to lift her off the toilet and get her back to her room, which was distressing to both of us. We put a commode by her bedside so that she could try to use the toilet there, without having to walk down the hall.

On one of Amy's visits during this time, Katie sat on the commode, while Amy stood behind her, supporting her and massaging her shoulders. Katie leaned back against Amy, and said, "You have *no idea* how frustrating this is to me." The loss of independence was so hard on her. We ordered a wheelchair just in case she needed one, but we kept it out of sight, in the garage, because seeing that would have upset Katie even more. It was not the kind of future that she wanted to contemplate.

I never slept with Katie, because she treasured her privacy; I never even suggested it. However, I began to worry that she might die alone in the night, and that I would come into her room some morning to find that she had passed away. This fear haunted me, but I felt that she wanted her privacy more than she wanted company, and I wanted to honor as many of her wishes as possible. Having the baby monitor (in case she called for us) would have to do.

A week after Andrea and Mike's wedding, Katie became paralyzed from the waist down. The way we found this out was when Katie tried to get up out of bed to use the commode. She slowly slid to the edge of her bed, waiting a long time to stand up. I was in her room, waiting to assist her, and I looked away for a moment. During that moment, she stood up next to her bed, and her legs buckled beneath her. There was no strength or control left, because the tumor was pressing on her spinal nerve. It hurt me to watch her lie in her bed, trying to get her legs to move, and then trying to move them by using her hands. It was heartbreaking, seeing her losing one more freedom.

Katie & Latte, August, 2007

At that point, we could tell that she was really "***done;***" it was obvious to us that she was disgusted at what her life was becoming. It was falling so far short of her expectations. I wonder if that gave her peace about facing death.

After her terminal diagnosis, Katie asked me what I thought it was like when we die. I said, "I don't know, because I have not been there; I've read about it, and what I've read is that it's peaceful and beautiful, and we will be greeted by people who love us, who we love. I believe that we go on from here - that our lives go on in another form."

I told her, "When Dad and I wanted to have you, I asked God if we could have another child, and you arrived. I believe that you came from Love, and I think you're going back to that Love. That's what I believe." She didn't ask any more after that; that answer seemed to satisfy her.

Katie didn't seem to be frightened of dying; she didn't want to die, but she was clearly fed up with the condition of her body. With the necessary increase in pain medication, Katie was drowsy much of the time, and she slept more. She began to sweat, and she experienced double-vision. These were new symptoms to report to Amy, and I asked her, privately, what they meant. Amy simply said that they were part of the "disease process."

Not knowing what course such a rare disease would take was like traveling in a foreign country without a map. Having Amy – a highly experienced nurse - as a guide was priceless in helping me to stay calm and navigate through whatever happened to Katie. No matter what happened, I wanted Katie to feel safe and loved, and that meant doing my best not to communicate fear or worry to her. In order to do that, I had to let go of my natural dread of her passing, and just remain in the moment as much as possible.

Katie wanted cable television in her room, so we called the cable company and bought a TV with a DVD player in it for her. The cable installer didn't arrive on the day he was supposed to come, and while we were waiting for him, my dear friend Maribeth came to visit. Katie was very drowsy, watching movies and TV, sleeping on and off. Maribeth leaned over Katie's bed, wearing a beautiful long necklace. Katie's eyes were closed; then she opened them, looked up, touched the necklace, and said drowsily to Maribeth, "You're *such* a disappointment to me." Maribeth was alarmed and asked, in a tiny voice, "I am?" to which Katie replied, "Yes; you're *supposed* to be the cable guy." That is a very fond memory that we still laugh about. The next day, the cable guy arrived, and Katie got her cable connection.

> *No matter what happened, I wanted Katie to feel safe and loved, and that meant doing my best not to communicate fear or worry to her...I had to let go of my natural dread of her passing, and remain in the moment as much as possible.*

An illustration of how much Katie loved her privacy is a story one of her friends - an older girlfriend (Maribeth's daughter), Taylor – told us. Tay would come to visit, and the girls would lie on Katie's bed and watch movies together. They would nap and talk, too. I had to go in periodically throughout the day to give Katie her medication, and I would do this as unobtrusively as possible. One day when Tay was there, I went in to take care of something for Katie. Tay told me later that, after I walked out of the room, Katie looked at her, rolled her eyes and said quietly, *"They're driving me crazy."* She had a funny, sassy attitude, which we all loved.

When her cousins were visiting one evening, Katie had been sweating, so she had a damp washcloth on her forehead to help her feel cool and comfortable. She wanted it to be refreshed with cool water, so Mike offered to take care of that. Katie told him, "No; you're a guest. Watch *this*," and she called into the baby monitor loudly, *"MO-OM!"* I came running, not knowing why she was yelling for me. She very calmly handed the washcloth to me to refresh. When I told this story to Maribeth later, she laughed and said, imitating Katie's voice, "Watch me make her dance on the head of a pin!" Even when bedridden, Katie had fun wherever she could find it.

After she became paralyzed, I couldn't turn Katie over in bed by myself. She had to wear disposable undergarments, and I could not change them for her without help. At that point, I asked Gregg to take a leave of absence from his job to help me take care of Katie. We had no idea what was coming or how long she would be in this condition. Amy came to help every few days, each week, for a short time, but I couldn't lift Katie or turn her (to avoid bed sores) on my own, so Gregg did take a leave from his job.

The first day of Gregg's leave was August 16th; it was a sunny morning. I went into Katie's room and found that it was a bit chilly, so I started to close her window. She looked directly at me from her bed and said clearly, "I need that open." I re-opened the window.

David planned to go cycling with my father that day, so I said to him, "Why don't you spend a little time with your sister before you go out?" I knew that he would be away for most of the day. David asked Katie if he could trim his fingernails in her bedroom, and she said that he could. He started clipping them into a wastebasket, and she looked at him and said, "I changed my mind; that's bothering me. You'll have to stop." David left the room; Katie was giving very clear directions.

Gregg and I came into the room to change her undergarment. Because she had no sensation below the waist, she had no awareness of whether she had had a bowel movement or was wet. It was important to keep her clean to avoid a rash or bedsores. As we were changing her undergarment, we had to turn her a bit, and she said to us quietly, "When you do that, it makes it hard to breathe." We immediately laid her back down on the pillows, and gave her a bolus of morphine (which helps with breathing issues). We asked if she was in any pain, and she said "No." We asked if she could breathe easily, and she said "Yes," so we finished the job as best we could, with as little movement to her as possible.

> *Katie looked directly at me and said, "You stay with me."*

Maribeth came over to deliver a prescription. I didn't come downstairs to greet her, because I was watching Katie to be sure she was all right. Gregg answered the door, and was talking to Maribeth, when I noticed that Katie's breathing was changing. I called out to Gregg to come upstairs, so Maribeth left quickly, and Gregg came up the stairs. We sat watching her, and then Katie looked directly at me and said, *"You stay with me."*

I lay down next to her on the bed. Her eyes were closed, so I asked her if she could feel me next to her, and she said "Yes." Katie had a damp washcloth on her brow, and I noticed drops of sweat on her chest, so I began to dab the sweat on her chest with the cloth. She didn't open her eyes, but she said, "I need that *here*," tapping her brow, so I put it back on her brow and lay quietly next to her.

Katie's arms were crossed over her chest, and although I would have loved to hold her in my arms, I had the sense that she was *working*. I don't know how else to explain it; the only word I can use is "working." She was breathing easily, and slowly; not laboriously nor struggling, but she looked as if she was engaged in an inner experience, and I didn't want to break into that, so I just lay close to her. I wanted her to feel my presence, as I had promised her I would be with her every step of her journey.

At this point, Gregg and David were sitting on the other side of her bed; we were quietly watching her. Katie opened her eyes wide, closed them again, and started to whisper. For a moment, I panicked, because I couldn't clearly hear what she was saying; I was worried that she wanted me to do something, or that she needed something from me, and I could not hear what it was. I put my ear very close to her mouth, and heard her say "It's been two years," or "Two years ago." She continued breathing very slowly, gently, then slower, slower…and then she stopped breathing.

Gregg and David and I looked at each other in disbelief – what just happened? Was that it? Had Katie just died? It did not sound final, but she hadn't taken another breath. We got a mirror to see if her breath would create a mist upon it, because we couldn't feel her pulse - we couldn't feel anything. We felt like bumbling idiots, and started laughing at ourselves through our tears. We said to Katie, "Sorry, honey – you know us! *The Keystone Cops!*" There was no misting on the mirror, no discernable pulse, so Gregg called Amy and said, "We think Katie just passed away; can you please come?" We were in shock.

That is how Katie died. There was no appearance of pain; there was no struggle. There was no need for the medications in the refrigerator, thanks be to God. There was no warning; she just said to me, *"You stay with me."* I know she trusted my promise to be with her to the end; perhaps that's why she said it. It was my privilege to be asked to lie next to her while she passed, and yet I had a great sense that this was a private, individual transition and that I wasn't to interfere.

> *I had a strong sense that this was a private, individual transition and that I wasn't to interfere.*

We never asked her to "fight cancer;" we never asked her *not to die*. We tried to make it easy for her, and I'm very grateful that she died without any appearance of pain, struggle or fear. She simply passed on, out of her body.

> *We never asked her to "fight cancer;" we never asked her not to die.*

Amy arrived and confirmed to us that Katie was indeed dead. She asked me if I wanted her to remove Katie's NG tube, and I said "yes," so she did that. I also told her that I wanted to wash Katie's body, and asked her to help me, as this was a new experience for me.

We took one of Katie's favorite scented soaps and washed her body with it, and changed her clothes. I rubbed lotion on her skin, and cut a lock of her hair. Amy notified the funeral director – they had to take Katie away at some point - while I dressed Katie in one of her favorite outfits, her "going away from home" clothes.

I put her in a shirt which I had never liked – one that Katie chose on a shopping expedition with her aunt. It was a camouflage tank-top with a rhinestone skull and crossbones on it, and though I disliked that tank top, I thought it was a good way to strike back at death – to send our daughter to the funeral home wearing a skull and crossbones made of rhinestones. She wore her brown gaucho pants and that tank-top. Katie had started the "gaucho style" trend at her elementary school, so it seemed right.

I remember watching as Amy poured all of Katie's remaining medications down the drain in the kitchen sink. I thought one would simply toss them into the garbage can, but controlled substances must be disposed of according to regulations.

Sadly, on the day she died, I had to remove the rings that my parents and I had given to Katie from her fingers; that was a very hard, final thing to have to do. Now, I have them, and I don't know what their future is.

My spiritual director came to the house, and brought a rose for Katie. She put it in Katie's hands, and we sat in her bedroom on the window seat for hours, while Katie lay on her bed, before the funeral director arrived. The wind was coming from the South that day. We could see the clouds moving from South to North in the blue expanse of sky, and yet while Bev and I were sitting in Katie's room, the wind came in through the North window, many times. It rustled all of the pictures and posters on the walls of Katie's room, went around the room, and then it would die down. Again and again, it came from the North and moved everything on the walls and died down.

After this happened about a half-dozen times, we noticed and remarked about how strange it was. Gregg came into Katie's room, and we pointed it out to him – and he saw it, too. Amy told me later that in the old days, nurses would always open a window in the room of a dying person, to allow their spirit to leave. I have a sense that it was Katie's spirit, while her body was still on the bed, telling us that she was free. As if she was saying to us, "Look at me; I'm not in there (her body) anymore; I'm free!" It was definitely not just the wind, because the wind was coming from the opposite direction.

A couple of nights later, I had an experience when I felt Katie's spirit with me. I read about this later in a book by Elisabeth Kubler-Ross; it is apparently a well-documented phenomenon that many people have observed after the death of someone important to them. I had not yet read about it at the time this happened to me - I read about it afterwards.

I was lying in bed with Gregg, crying uncontrollably, and was trying to catch my breath. After I stopped crying, I saw a multicolored ball of light, like a bunch of sparklers' tips, floating down the hall towards our bedroom. The bedroom door was open, and the ball came floating into the room. I asked Gregg, "Can you see that? That ball? It is coming into our room," but he couldn't see it. It floated over to the bed, but Gregg said he still didn't see it. I watched this ball of light hover over our bed. It was a constantly-moving ball, comprised of sparks of light - different colors of light, with open space between them.

Katie knew that Gregg has trouble finding things – for example, he couldn't find the mustard in the refrigerator, even if it was right in front of him – and as the ball of light came over to the bed, it moved right next to the tip of Gregg's nose, which was something Katie would have done, as if to say, "Can you see me now? I'm right in front of you!" I felt as if I could hear her spirit - the essence of her - talking to us. Gregg still couldn't see this ball of light, though it was at the tip of his nose, so I said, laughing through my tears, "Oh, Honey - you know he can't find anything!"

After that, the ball moved between us, came up in front of my face and hovered there. I watched until it disappeared, and was comforted by what I felt was Katie's presence. Later, I read about this phenomenon in the book _On Life After Death_ by Kubler-Ross. On page 62, she describes how the spirit - energy – manifests in this form. It is beautiful and comforting to think that Katie is able to be with us in this way, and I've looked for her in other ways since then. I haven't looked for Katie's body or her physical form, but I see her presence in sparks of light, in butterflies, in feelings – a variety of different ways, unexpected, and always a gift - since she has been gone physically.

CHAPTER 8:

The Path of Grieving

We held Katie's Celebration of Life in a beautiful lodge near our home, where she had hoped to have her wedding reception (see Appendix A). It was filled to overflowing – hundreds of people came to hear our cousin, Kim, give Katie's eulogy, to hear Bev's inspirational talk and to watch the slideshow of Katie's life. Gregg, a quiet man, stunned me with his courage in standing up and addressing the crowd at the beginning of the event. Bev shared with our guests the words I had said to her about Katie's journey: "We didn't get what we asked for; we got what we needed."

We planned it as a party, according to Katie's directions. We served smoked salmon, hors d'oeuvres, beverages and cakes. The lodge sits among acres of lawn, trees and flowers; it has a long stretch of sandy beach, with paths for walking, garden areas to explore and pavilions for relaxing. The place was in full summer bloom, the night was warm, and the fireworks which Katie requested exploded against the starry sky. The receiving line literally never ended.

It was not our desire to receive flowers as condolences, so we asked my brother to contact the hospital and deal with the formalities of setting up an endowment for cancer research in Katie's name. He very kindly took care of this. When the time came to write Katie's obituary, we requested that people donate to the Katie Gerstenberger Endowment for Cancer Research at Seattle Children's Hospital. It grew quickly, and its income now helps to fund solid tumor research, in accordance with Katie's desires. As of this writing, the principal amount is over $163,000.

> *"We didn't get what we asked for; we got what we needed."*

Scattering Katie's ashes in Puget Sound at Camp Goodtimes West

We scattered her ashes, which was both painful and powerful. It was beautiful to carry out her wishes, but terribly hard to let go of her physical remains, so I kept some of her ashes.

There is very little that you can do to help when a child knows that she is dying, but when you are able to grant any of her wishes - even in the matter of where to scatter her remains, it feels right to do it – and taking those steps can help people in the process of grieving. However, they are bittersweet steps, and in our case, it took years before we were able to complete Katie's request.

I will never forget hearing my father say about Katie (his only granddaughter), his voice breaking, "I was in love with the girl." He couldn't remember his own son-in-law's name at Katie's Celebration of Life; he was utterly bereft. Gregg's mother could not even attend the memorial service. Her closest sister had died in May, and her granddaughter in August; she was literally ill with grief.

It has been hard for us to watch our parents – Katie's grandparents, in their 70s and 80s – suffer so much in their grief. Katie's death also precipitated a spiritual crisis for some family members. One of them told me that he delivered an ultimatum to God at the outset of Katie's illness: "If this doesn't go well, we are through"...and it *didn't* go well. I know that our parents suffered watching us endure with Katie, just as Gregg and I felt anguish watching David and Katie suffer. The older generation's suffering was, in a sense, doubled with Katie's illness and death.

I don't cry easily. While Katie was ill, I had to learn to do many things that I didn't want to do, holding my emotions in check, when what I really wanted to do was to run screaming from the building. That wasn't an option, so I developed a tight self-control to avoid breaking down in front of others. Occasionally, I now suffer from panic attacks, and I can't do certain things that I used to do.

When I was David's age, I climbed 14,000-foot peaks, went white-water rafting and rode horses on mountain trails and in rodeo events; I traveled in Europe. I was not a fearful person. I deeply dislike the fact that the trauma comes back and hits me at random, knocking the breath out of me; it is a harsh side effect of the cancer journey. It can be embarrassing, and it makes me feel a bit feeble – but I am not feeble; I have simply been traumatized. It is necessary to remind myself of that fact, and to be gentle, rather than judgmental about it.

Some parents have told me that the thing they hated the most on this journey was signing the consent forms to their child's treatment, which detail all of the possible side effects, including death, or permanent impairment. I tried to look at Katie's treatment notebook last year – I was looking for something in the hospital paperwork - and when I found the notebook, I literally fell to my knees on the floor; I couldn't open it. I felt nauseous and short of breath; there's a visceral response to these memories. I don't cry often, but my grief comes out in other ways.

Talking and writing about Katie is a comfort for me, because I miss her so much and love to go over my memories of all of her life, treasuring the moments we shared. Gregg and David do not like to discuss her and reminisce as much as I do, so writing is a release and a way to honor my own desires, without dishonoring Gregg's and David's.

There are some interesting studies about posttraumatic stress disorder in parents of critically ill children. The studies of post-traumatic stress disorder in parents of children who've had cancer, and studies of parents of children who have disabilities, or who have had a lot of hospitalizations, show that rhythmic exercises are helpful. Some people use a cross-country ski machine or treadmill to get this effect. I walk every day, between three and six miles.

By the time she died, Katie was my best friend. I am not a woman who looks to her children to fulfill a "buddy" role in her life; however, Katie and I went through so much together that no one else experienced – the two of us were a team, nearly every minute of the day, during her illness. Through those shared experiences, we both matured and changed, and we just grew into each other. Gregg and I enjoy a close, fulfilling and happy marriage, yet Katie and I grew as close as I've ever been to anyone. It's not that I love her more than David or Gregg; we simply became very intimately connected over the last 10 months of her life.

In the first weeks after Katie's passing, I slept with her comforter – the one which I had made for her. She had held onto that quilt all through her treatment and recovery; you can see it in many of our photographs. If I needed to wash it, I had to return it to her on the same day. There are two kinds of fabric in it, and she preferred to have it on her bed with a certain side up. She loved that quilt, and used it as a real *comforter* all through her cancer journey: as a mask, a bathrobe, a blinder, a hiding place, a lap robe, a privacy screen. After she died, sleeping with her quilt felt like a link to her, physically.

I started to think about what that quilt meant to me, and the idea of sewing simple quilts for other cancer patients began to take shape in my mind. I asked two of my dearest friends, both of whom know how to sew, for help.

We devised a simple pattern, and sewed the first quilt. When I could not seem to motivate myself to do anything, I would think of patients like Katie, and their families, and get up off the couch to sew – to bring comfort to them. Later, I decided I needed help with this project, because I wanted to expand it to include all wards of the hospital, so I founded **Katie's Comforters Guild at Seattle Children's Hospital.** We make quilts and blankets for all newly-admitted patients. At the time of this writing, we have more than 50 members, and have donated hundreds of quilts. If you would like more information, please go to www. katiescomfortersguild.blogspot.com.

Initially following Katie's passing, it was hard for me to move off of our cozy yellow couch. Even grocery shopping in our small community felt hazardous. The looks, the stares, the way people responded to me in public made me want to stay at home. I could see from the looks in their eyes – usually pity or fear - that we represented their worst nightmare, and for a while, those looks intimidated me. I refused to go to the store on my own for many months.

Writing my blog was therapeutic for me, and it allowed me to express whatever I was feeling without the danger of wearing other people out with my emotions. No one has to read it, but I can say whatever I need to say without fear. I've received great encouragement through blogging; my grief-community and creative community have grown tremendously, enriching my life and bringing comfort. I've met many other bereaved parents and parents of children with special needs.

I've been asked to speak to groups in various places, to write a column for an online community; my words have been published in newspapers and magazines. Raising awareness and funds for research, encouraging others along the way, has given purpose and meaning to my days in the midst of the black hole of this terrible loss.

My spiritual path has deepened and grown through Katie's illness and her death; the story of that path, much of which is detailed on my blog (www.karengberger.blogspot.com) could fill a book all on its own.

The last thing I see before going to sleep at night is a sort of "altar" which I assembled by my bedside. Some of Katie's ashes are in a heart-shaped urn. There are photos and figurines which are symbolic of our love, and that mother-child bond, which is unbreakable…even in death.

Often, a song will express my feelings better than I could in my own words. There have been many songs that I have sung through tears – tears of truth, tears of understanding, tears of sorrow, tears of love. Jackson Browne's "Sky Blue & Black," R.E.M.'s "It's the End of the World," and Tree 63's "Blessed Be Your Name," are just a few examples.

Each year since Katie's passing has been different, and I daresay each year will be, since grief is a process, and we change with it. The first year was characterized by intense, relentless pain. The loss was always at the forefront of our minds, crushing our hearts. There were physical symptoms: pain in the left side of the torso, chest pain, lethargy, numbness. There were also emotional symptoms, such as depression and a muffling of day to day feelings, along with tears and wondering if we could actually survive this pain. It was difficult to move in society; even simple things, like shopping for groceries, were difficult. There were spiritual side effects, such as anger, questioning and arguments with God, as well as a deep desire to rest in Him.

We found that we grieved differently from one another, male and female, parents and sibling. Our loss is different, our relationships with Katie are unique, and our personalities are distinct. We process our pain differently, and we cannot necessarily comfort each other very well. A way in which this was very clear was on "anniversary" days: Katie's diagnosis, her surgery, her birthday, and on the anniversary of her passing. We each had different feelings about these days and how to mark them, and that has made those days even more painful and difficult for each of us.

The pain impacted our thoughts, our behavior and all of our relationships. I wrote on my blog about that pain, during the first few months after Katie died:

"I spend a lot of time in pain these days, so I have been thinking about the subject.

"Many days include the sensation of pain in my chest –in my heart, actually. Heartache. It feels as if someone has run me through with his sword, and the pain goes all the way through to my back.

"The pain of emptiness is new to me. I have a full life, and many interests. I never thought that the death of one person would make me feel so empty, and that the emptiness would be not a blank or negative space, but an aching longing. Sometimes I feel as if I am made of ashes; sometimes, like an old, honeycombed-beehive, tissue-papery, gray, flaking away in pieces. Dead, in a way…or perhaps just dormant?

"I miss Katie so much that it hurts, literally. I miss her qualities and her way of looking at things, her sweet softness and her spiciness. I ache deeply over the things that will never be: the school days, sharing her learning, the vacations, weekends together, the dances, the dreams never to be pursued, the love –perhaps a wedding and babies, watching her mature, and the maturing of our relationship. I hurt when I think of the loss to David of his best friend and lifelong buddy; he will not have an ally of his generation who 'gets' all of the things that are unique about his upbringing, someone to share those memories (and the griping about the 'old folks' –Gregg and me– that is often a way of coping with aging parents).

"Those of you who have given birth to a baby know a kind of intense pain. I had no idea such pain existed on this

earth, until I had my first baby (David); it was the awaken-
ing of a very naive woman. When I learned in my own body
about that suffering, I was shocked and mystified. It took a
long time for me to integrate that into my being. I remember
my sister asking me what labor felt like, and my answer: 'It
felt as if someone was prying my body open with a crowbar.'

"They tried to prepare us for it in childbirth classes; they
said to focus on your breathing. I found that impossible, at
that time in my life. In those days, I fought pain. Now, after
doing some reading of Buddhist writings over the years, I see
that there is another path: being present to the pain, with
acceptance and openness. It is terrifying, at first, but it is a
better path, for me.

"The physical pain of this grieving is surprising to me.
Perhaps that is why it is so exhausting, and why I have not
enough energy (or social patience) to go out or be with many
people. It is not the right time for me. This time needs to be
devoted to surfing these storm waves of pain, and keeping
myself from drowning in them.

"There are memories in my mind of the past year and
a half that are traumatic. They cause sharp pain. I carry
mental images that hurt me, yet they are some of the last ones
I have of my life with my daughter. I never want to lose a
memory of Katie, but some of them are hard to live with, all
the same.

"Watching my daughter suffer created pain in me.
Watching her bravely receive daily injections (two and three
times a day), holding her hand through countless scans,
blood draws, infusions, procedures; holding her as she vom-
ited many times a day; medicating her around the clock;
holding her as she cried out in pain, and being unable to
relieve it immediately; helping her in ways too intimate and

numerous to detail...memories of her suffering are part of my suffering. Yet, in caring for her, I found my deepest personal joy. I could just be *my love for her, and this is the greatest work I have ever been privileged to do.*

"*Caring for a person you love who is dying is a journey through a landscape of the mind and body that I cannot describe fully. It is both painful and beautiful –not unlike giving birth, contradictory in its nature. Unlike giving birth, however, it is not a beginning, full of hope, for the caregiver. Perhaps it may be for the one who dies, moving away from us into another life, but for those left behind, it is a desolate and painful leave-taking, no matter how gentle the dying may be.*

"*I find myself longing to be back with her on any day, even in the hospital, even when she was dying at home, yet I do not wish for her to suffer any longer. As hard as it was to suffer with her, I would just love to have one more moment, one more hour, one more day with that wonderful, joyful, fascinating girl who lit up my life.*"

On the first anniversary of Katie's admission to the hospital, I wrote on my blog:

"*The world has become a darker place, for me, yet I learned and saw many important things along the way. The worst thing I learned, at least as I see it today, is that you can work as hard as you know how to work, with all of the experts and expertise available, with the best of intentions, surrounded by good will in amounts that you never dreamed possible, with a love so great that it's hard to believe it flows through one human heart, and you may still have to watch your child suffer and die. That is why the world looks so different to me now; that, and the fact that the light of one lovely, feisty, gorgeous, hilarious, spritely, creative 12-year-old girl is no longer with me in this place."*

Closing Katie's bank account hurt my heart; it was harder still when the teller became tearful. Carrying out Katie's wishes – fulfilling the directions in her will, where she stipulated that certain belongings should go to certain charities – was rewarding, but painful. Going into her room was comforting; however, opening her closet or dresser could cause terrible grief. The pain was very unpredictable.

The second year was marked by the wearing off of the shock of Katie's passing. This meant we felt everything more strongly. I remember around the first anniversary of Katie's passing (the beginning of "year two") when we were on a weekend vacation with family and friends out in the country. We had a barbecue and gathered to eat and visit with all of the children, from college age to babies. I realized, as I listened to all of the lively conversations, that Katie would never grow up with these children; she would never grow older than 12 and a half. The other children would go through ages, stages and rites of passage, but Katie would not.

As I lay in bed that night, harsh sobs came, as hard as the night after she died. It struck me in a new, raw way that *she is never coming back*. Time did not feel as if it was healing anything at all; on the contrary, some of the pain of missing her was more intense the second year, because of the loss of the numbness of shock. This was in itself a bit of a surprise. There were days when we felt as if we were doing okay, and suddenly, we "hit a pothole" or "fell in a pit" of grief, and found ourselves stunned and hurting afresh, as if a partially-healed wound had broken open. We were also healing in different ways from one another, and this sometimes created tension, or a feeling of being out of step.

One day, when Gregg was in tears of grief, I took David aside and spoke to him about it. He said, with wisdom beyond his years, "I feel sorry for you and Dad. I have my whole life ahead of me; I can have a family of my own, but your family is complete – this is it. I feel sorry that it's so hard for you." His understanding and empathy were deep, and they gave me assurance that he was going to survive this.

An excerpt from my blog, during the second year after Katie's passing:

"I decided a while ago that I was going to tell the truth about my grief journey here. As if I were a reporter from the front lines of some horrendous battlefield, I would tell it as it is happening. This week, the grief is raw and fresh as an open wound, and I would be lying if I pretended it wasn't.

"Here is a bit of truth from the front lines: it's been said that the second year after the death of a child is actually worse than the first, for some people. The shock has worn off, and that shock is a powerful buffer. Friends, this is true for me, here and now.

"…there is nothing we can do, get, change or make, that is going to make this situation go away. NOTHING. We cannot buy, sell, move, eat, drink, run, divorce, conceive, adopt, exchange, 'beg, borrow or

steal' our way out of this heartache. It is where we live now…

"We spent the majority of our time and resources investing in [our family], spending time together, loving, teaching, sharing, building a healthy and happy home, nurturing our children and our family as a whole, as a unit, as a foursome. We will never on this earth be that foursome again. One of our members has been stolen away. She is gone, and we are not whole.

"…It is a hard place to be, and it is hard to witness your beloved in that kind of pain.

"We still have our love for one another; we cannot lose love. We have our dear son David. We have a roof over our heads, food in the cupboards, a warm bed to sleep in…I still love God and I know that God loves us. But this one treasure, this precious family, is broken to bits, and it will never be the same again."

The third year has been better for us. Joy is returning. Life is enjoyable; we are pursuing our interests again. Through practice, my gratitude for all that is in our lives has become stronger. This gives me reason to hope, and the desire to share that hope with others. We are growing accustomed to living with the loss, living without Katie, but we are not going to "get over it." We are learning to live with the "Katie-shaped hole" in our lives.

All of this has happened because a 12-year old girl lived and died with such courage, integrity, hilarity, sadness and real-ness that she still inspires us every day. The loss, growth, heartbreak, heart-expanding, awareness, fundraising, learning, and so much more – all of this is *because of Katie.*

Timeline

September, 2006: Virus symptoms, clinic visits, tests

October   Admission to Seattle Children's Hospital on October 10. Biopsy & tentative diagnosis on Oct. 13: neuroblastoma. Begin chemotherapy in ICU. Move to SCCA ward. David transfers to Hutch School.

November   Second biopsy; round #2 of chemotherapy changed to target adrenocortical carcinoma; finished on Nov. 12. Move to Ronald McDonald House (when Katie is outpatient). Thanksgiving celebrated there. Clots/tumor spots in lungs dissolve. Chemo round #3 begins on Nov. 28.

December   Chemotherapy round #3. Outpatient weeks at Ronald McDonald House. Go home for several days. Fever and need for transfusions cause inpatient stay between rounds of chemo. Chemotherapy round #4. Christmas Day in hospital and Ronald McDonald House.

January, 2007 Transfusions of platelets and red blood cells needed. Mouth sores (in throat). Go home. Last round (#5) of inpatient chemotherapy. Recover from chemotherapy.

February   Recover from chemotherapy. Meet with surgeons about procedure to remove her tumor. Home for 3 weeks.

February 21 – 22   Surgery

March   Recovery from surgery. Incision fully closed by Dr. Waldhausen on March 6. Katie turns 12 in CICU on March 8. Breathing tube removed March 13. Move out of CICU to surgical recovery ward on March 14. March 24: all remaining surgical drains (and some stitches) removed.

March 30   Katie attends blood drive held in her honor.

April   Released from hospital for good on April 1! Recovery. Last of stitches removed. PICC line removed. CT scan results: unchanged.

May   Mother's day and commuting to Hutch School. PET scan at Univ. of WA. Gets ears pierced. Begin registration for public school in autumn. Katie begins Mitotane

	therapy (oral chemo, taken at home).
June	School year ends; Father's Day. Register Katie for BPA drama camp. David & Katie spend a week at Camp Goodtimes West.
July	Invited to be a bridesmaid in cousin's wedding, scheduled for February 2008. Katie experiences leg and back pain, weakness and nausea. Speak at Steve Pool-Warren Moon Guild event.
July 20	CT scan reveals relapse. No further options for treatment. Begin Hospice care.
August 2	Katie and David are attendants in wedding.
August 9	Katie becomes paralyzed from the waist down.
August 16	Katie passes away.

Epilogue: Spiritual Journey

"If there is anywhere on earth a lover of God who is always kept safe, I know nothing of it, for it was not shown to me. But this was shown: that in falling and rising again we are always kept in that same precious love." – Julian of Norwich

As mentioned at the beginning of this book, I am fortunate to be engaged in a profession that allows me to devote time and energy to my spiritual path. This path is an ecumenical one, embracing teachings from a variety of spiritual traditions, though my background is Christian. I have been blessed by many books, classes and teachers from Buddhist, Catholic, Jewish, Protestant, Quaker and Sufi roots. From my perspective, the mystical part of these traditions is the one that speaks a similar message of love, and so I am drawn to the mystics and their insight. The following passages have helped to light my path.

The journey through cancer with a loved one, child or adult, is to me much like being in the belly of a whale (the imagery is from a story about Jonah, from the Old Testament in the Bible). Richard Rohr, a Franciscan priest and founder of the Center for Action and Contemplation wrote an insightful piece about it:

"It demands that we release ourselves into the belly of darkness before we can know what is essential. It insists that the spiritual journey is more like giving up control than taking control. It might even be saying that…we will get to the right shore by God's grace more than right action on our part…

"Jonah knew what God was doing, and how God does it, and how right God is—only *after* emerging from the belly of the whale. He has no message whatsoever to give until he has first endured the journey, the darkness, the spitting up on the right shore—all in spite of his best efforts to avoid these very things… Jesus had found the Jonah story inspiring, no doubt, because it described almost perfectly what was happening to him!"
- From Wondrous Encounters: Scripture for Lent, pp. 31-32, by Richard Rohr, St. Anthony Messenger Press

Prayer (adapted from Joyce Rupp)
God, we thank You for the gift of Katie.
You know what a treasure she has been for us.
It is painful to part with her physical presence.
Bless the hurt in our hearts as we trudge through each day.
Grace us with awareness of your loving presence each moment of our lives.

"In a world so torn apart by rivalry, anger, and hatred, we have the privileged vocation to be living signs of a love that can bridge all divisions and heal all wounds." *-Henri Nouwen*

"Do not look forward to what may happen tomorrow; the same everlasting Father who cares for you today will take care of you tomorrow and every day. Either He will shield you from suffering, or He will give you unfailing strength to bear it. Be at peace, then. Put aside all anxious thoughts and imaginations, and say continually: "The Lord is my strength and my shield. My heart has trusted in Him and I am helped. He is not only with me but in me, and I in Him." -*St. Francis de Sales*

"The Spirit helps us in our weakness. For when we do not know what to say in prayer, the Spirit expresses what we mean in wordless sounds and sighs." -*Romans 8:26*

"Prayer isn't bending God's arms in order to get things, or talking God into things. God is already totally given. Prayer is us learning how to receive, learning how to wait, listen, possess something. It's not that we pray and God answers; our praying is already God answering. Your desire to pray is God in your heart. Your reaching out to enter into dialogue with the Lord is already the answer of God. It is grace that makes us desire grace."
- *Richard Rohr, Radical Grace, p. 172*

"We love you, O our God; and we desire to love you more and more. Grant to us that we may love you as much as we desire, and as much as we ought. O dearest friend, who has so loved and saved us, the thought of whom is so sweet and always growing sweeter, come with Christ and dwell in our hearts; that you keep a watch over our lips, our steps, our deeds, and we shall not need to be anxious either for our souls or our bodies. Give us love, sweetest of all gifts, which knows no enemy. Give us in our hearts pure love, born of your love to us, that we may love others as you love us. O most loving Father of Jesus Christ, from whom flows all love, let our hearts, frozen in sin, cold to you and cold to others, be warmed by this divine fire. So help and bless us in your Son." *-Prayer of Anselm, 12th century.*

"IN DESPERATE hope I go and search for her in all the corners of my room; I find her not.

My house is small and what once has gone from it can never be regained.

But infinite is thy mansion, my lord, and seeking her I have come to thy door.

I stand under the golden canopy of thine evening sky and I lift my eager eyes to thy face.

I have come to the brink of eternity from which nothing can vanish - no hope, no happiness, no vision of a face seen through tears.

Oh, dip my emptied life into that ocean, plunge it into the deepest fullness. Let me for once feel that lost sweet touch in the allness of the universe."
- Rabindranath Tagore, Gitanjali, v. 87

More about the spiritual journey can be found here, and elsewhere on my blog:
www.karengberger.blogspot.com/2011/02/random-thoughts-on-religion-faith.html

Celebrating Katie's Life

August 22, 2007, Kiana Lodge, Poulsbo, WA (led by Beverly Gaines)

Katie led a wonderful life for most of her 12$^{1/2}$ years. Honoring her wishes, we hosted a party to celebrate her life in the place where she wanted to have her wedding reception, on a starry August night. Hundreds of people attended.

"Let us take a few moments to drop down into that place of stillness to meet and encounter the love of God. As we open our hearts and minds to God's presence, I'll be opening with the Lord's Prayer (from the New Zealand Prayer book):

Eternal Spirit, Earth-maker, Pain-bearer, Life-giver,
Source of all that is and that shall be,
Father and Mother of us all,
Loving God, in who is heaven;
The hallowing of your name echo through the universe!
The way of your justice be followed by the peoples of the world!
Your heavenly will be done by all created beings!
Your commonwealth of peace and freedom sustain our hope
and come on earth.
With the bread we need for today, feed us.
In the hurts we absorb from one another, forgive us.
In times of temptation and test, strengthen us.
From trials too great to endure, spare us.
From the grip of all that is evil, free us.
For you reign in the glory of the power that is Love,
Now and forever.

"We thank you for this time of gathering to re-member, honor and celebrate the life of Katie. Help us to be open to this great love which we have seen and felt throughout this tragic experience. May your love guide us tonight as we share the joy and sorrow. May your touch be a healing balm on Katie's family and friends as we begin to live without her physical presence. Amen.

"In the New Testament, the 13th chapter of 1 Corinthians ends with this verse: "And now faith, hope, and love abide, these three and the greatest of these is love. "

"Faith … Frederick Buechner says, "Faith is better understood as verb than as a noun, as a process than as a possession.""

- It is on-again-off-again rather than once-for-all.
- Faith is not being sure where you're going but going anyway.
- A journey without maps.
- Doubt isn't the opposite of faith; it is an element of faith.

"Father Richard Rohr (a favorite teacher/author of Karen's)– offers ideas on faith which helped to sustain her this last year –

- Belief is the intellectual assent and the emotional response of what we want to be true.
- We see the movement from belief to faith - it's about our letting go of the images we have of who God is, what life is supposed to be.
- Faith begins to grow in those in-between spaces where you're not sure you'll make it to second base.
- This is where faith happens - in the in-betweens, the interruptions, the thresholds.
- It happens when we leave the room where we were in control, where things made sense, and we understood what is happening and we move into a new room where everything is turned upside down and we recognize the many illusions we have been living with.
- Faith is born in the stripping away, in the surrendering of our dead certainties so that we can be open to what God is about in our lives.
- Faith grows from a real, immediate knowing that comes from experiencing God as the ground of our being, whose love is always flowing through everything that is.

- Rohr says, "Unless we can presume that the Holy One is speaking right now, how can we believe that God ever spoke? What if we proceed on the premise that God is acting and speaking in our lives right now."
- To have an attitude of faith then is to hear the Beloved speaking everywhere and all the time, in the concrete and the ordinary – in the tragic and joyful events of our lives.
- We realize this is the only real security there is in life and when we **experience this truth**, we feel loved.

"The prophet Isaiah in the Hebrew Scriptures offered these words from God to his community,

'Do not be afraid, for I have redeemed you, I have called you by name and you are mine. When you pass through the waters, I will be with you; and through the rivers, they shall not overwhelm you; when you walk through fire you shall not be burned, and the flame shall not consume you. You are precious in my sight and I love you. Do not fear for I am with you.'

"Beautiful words of faith.

"Hope:

- Hope serves as a companion when the future is unsure, unclear.
- Hope is not wishing – this is passive. Neither is hope just coping. Coping is just getting by.
- Hope remains open to all the possibilities, including the possibility that things may turn out

other than we imagined and that somehow it could still be well with our souls.

- Hope is essential to life; it is getting up one more time, giving ourselves one more chance.
- Hope sets our sail in difficult seas, or even becomes the anchor as we wait out a storm.
- With hope we can find meaning in how we respond to what has happened to us.
- In others words, with hope, whatever the outcome, we can go on.
- We see signs of hope in those who willingly risk, those who unselfishly give, those who courageously start over.
- Sometimes our hope is low, at the end of our rope and someone shows up in our life and becomes our *hope bearer*.
- Hope is not about moving mountains, it's about moving one single stone, and then another. One step at a time.
- Hoping with patience means living as fully as possible give the circumstances life has handed you.
- In Celebrating together, we recognize how hope has held us all together.
- Victor Frankl encountered hope while imprisoned in a WWII concentration camp. He later said he had survived those frightful conditions because of his great hope that he would be reunited with his wife, whom he often imagined was smiling and encouraging him to go on.
- When the war ended, he learned his wife had already died. While his grief was deep, he held

on to a sense of meaning. He wove her memories and her love into a new hope he created for his life. He hoped he could teach other to choose their own attitude toward what happens to them, just as he had learned to do. Eventually his hope came true and the book he wrote out of his experiences is considered very helpful for those low on hope ("Man's search for Meaning").

"A poem from Henri Nouwen captures this:

'Hope means to keep living

Amid desperation

And to keep humming

In the darkness.

Hoping is knowing that there is love,

It is trust in tomorrow

It is falling asleep

And waking again

When the sun rises.

In the midst of a gale at sea,

It is to discover land.

In the eyes of another

It is to see that she understands you.

As long as there is still hope

There will also be prayer

And God will be holding you

In God's hands.'

("With Open Hands" by Henry Nouwen)

Katie's Eulogy
(written and delivered by Kim Kristensen, Gregg's cousin)

"…On behalf of Gregg, Karen and David, it is my honor and pleasure to talk about Katie.

"I would like to first talk about the Gerstenbergers as a family this past year and second, about Katie - who she was and what made her special; for even though her life was short, Katie left an indelible impression. I hope all of us here will reflect upon her life and fondly remember the ever-smiling, vibrant little girl, who illuminated and enriched our lives for a short but brilliant moment.

The Gerty's – THE PIT CREW
"When Katie was diagnosed with cancer last October 13th, Gregg and Karen asked her what she wanted. Katie told them that she wanted the family to be together as much as possible. So David transferred from Poulsbo Junior High to the Hutch School (associated thru the Fred Hutchinson Cancer Center for cancer patients and their family members), to which he could commute from the hospital each day. Then the family moved to the Ronald McDonald House located next to the hospital to complete Katie's request. From there, at least one family member could be with her at all times, sleeping in her hospital room (with the exception of a short period in the ICU following her surgery – which made it practically impossible for

them to get any rest). They ate all their meals together, until chemo made the smell of food intolerable to her. Karen and Gregg helped the nurses. From that experience, they learned to give shots, medications, and to maintain her feeding tube and IV. They discussed the events of the day, and tried to live as much as possible as a normal family at home.

"This was very difficult for Gregg, Karen and David, but it was obviously the hardest on Katie. They became her "PIT CREW" – available 24/7, surrounding her with love and support every moment, because treating cancer and recovering from surgery is a relentless task.

"Many entries on CARINGBRIDGE'S website included accolades that described their bravery, strength and spirit. Many of those people openly questioned whether they possessed the wherewithal to endure Katie's illness, and the Gerstenberger family is to be admired and respected. However, Karen and Gregg didn't see it that way, for the logic of the accolades was confusing; to them their course was clear and simple: ask Katie what she wanted and do it. They did everything possible to become "THE PIT CREW" and make it happen. Katie was their daughter and you do everything humanly possible to help her survive.

"This is important because it shows the strength of their family: the love, compassion, and care that are the Gregg and Karen Gerstenberger family. For without Gregg and Karen, we cannot celebrate Katie's life, if we do not in the very least, celebrate the parents who created the warm and caring environment that nurtured Katie and she thrived in. It was where Katie became Katie.

Katie's Biography

"Kathryn Emilie Gerstenberger was born March 8th, 1995 in Seattle. She is the 9th and **youngest grandchild** of Ed and Elaine Gerstenberger, and the 3rd and **youngest grandchild** of Phil and Ellie Boren – their **only granddaughter.**

"Katie was a very happy, easy-going and healthy baby. She looked exactly like Gregg, so much so, that when Karen took his picture to her pediatrician, Diane Fuquay, she thought it was a picture of Katie.

"While Karen worked two days a week, Katie spent those days with Wendy Davenport until she was a year old; when she turned 1, she joined David at Maria (Ria) Norton's home daycare. Ria became like a 3rd grandmother to Gregg and Karen's children.

"One of Katie's special traits was how easily and effortlessly she made friends. After visits to Lion's Club Park in Poulsbo, she usually got in the car stating, "I made a new friend!" and proceeded to tell Gregg and Karen about the person. Katie never missed an opportunity to meet and play with someone and have fun. Katie loved life and reveled in it.

"She attended the Children's Garden Montessori School at Sawdust Hill Road, where she had her first crushes on boys (and vice-versa: "I can't be sick; I have to marry so & so on Thursday"). Even in preschool, she knew what she did and did not like. One of the teachers was determined to start her on reading some 'first' wordbooks, and Katie refused to cooperate. 'I HATE the "BoB" books!' she told us.

"Katie attended Poulsbo Elementary from Kindergarten to 5th grade. Her favorite subjects were reading & recess. She started 6th grade at West Sound Academy. At the onset of her illness, she had to withdraw. She finished the 6th grade at the Hutch School.

"While growing up, Katie had swimming, golf, tennis, piano, gymnastics and drama lessons. While she possessed natural athletic abilities, she sometimes disliked being enrolled in lessons. She did everything in her power, for example, to distract her piano teacher from their lessons, and tried to make her **laugh** as much as possible. Katie liked to learn but she also liked to enjoy things unfettered.

Things Katie Loved

Template: Walt Whitman, *I Hear America Singing*

"This poem describes the dynamics of a youthful and growing America – I believe it also reflects the same characteristic and attributes of Katie. So I used, *I Hear America Singing*, as a template to profile the youthful exuberance of Katie and the things she loved:

I Hear Katie Singing by Kim Kristensen

"I hear Katie singing, the varied carols I hear,

I see her playing and petting Latte & Liger, purring their happy sounds,

I see Katie having fun at family events & other parties, I hear her talking, laughing and loving everyone,

I see and hear Katie and David signing up with a talent agent, excitedly looking to the future,

I see and hear Katie rehearsing and performing for the Bainbridge Performing Arts Children's Theatre School,

I see Katie cautiously riding her scooter and bike,

I see Katie climbing and jumping from trees, her laughter echoing through the forest,

I hear Katie swinging & laughing on the rope swing Gregg & David built in their woods,

I see Katie combing the beach, rejoicing at each and every treasure she found,

I see Katie at a big crackling beach fire making s'mores and eating them with delight,

I see Katie playing with David at their grandparents' houses,

I see Katie boarding the jet to Palm Desert, anticipating the drive down Ramon Rd., playing at the pool and sitting in the hot tub, relishing the coming Pasta Night, shopping on El Paseo, going to the Marriott & La Quinta Grill,

I see the style-conscious Katie happily shopping for clothes, shoes, and jewelry,

I see and hear Katie's delight, picking fresh vegetables from Kappa's garden,

I see Katie quietly reading Nancy Drew and Louis Sachar stories or fashion magazines,

I see and hear Katie and David playing and making over the loft into Playmobil village,

I hear Katie scolding Liger for deconstructing their buildings and bring Playmobil items to Gregg and Karen,

I see Katie cheerfully being with her "Sitter-Sister," Angie Woodman,

I see Katie blissfully thumbing through family photo albums,

I see Katie people-watching, enjoying all those visual wonders,

I see Katie watching her favorite movies and TV shows: Harry Potter, Pirates of the Caribbean, PBS Mystery series and the Disney Channel,

I see and hear Katie laughing and playing with David – her brother & best friend,

I see Katie shooting baskets and dancing with her Dad, singing their joyous songs,

I see the last picture of the two beauties, Katie and Karen, and I sigh with nostalgia,

I hear Katie singing all her strong melodious songs, singing what belongs to her, no-one else, and I smile."

Katie's Funny Stories (from Karen's journal)

Watching the "Today Show"
The camera pans the crowd outside the studio. People wave, holding up placards with messages: "It's my birthday!" "From Iowa," "Florida Girls Love Matt" [Lauer, co-host]. They also shout greetings to people at home. One person says "Hi, Grandma!" and Katie yells back at the TV, "I am *not* your GRANDMA!" (*February 27, 1998*)

On the Beach
A man in a French bikini (thong) walks by Katie and Karen on the Agate Pass beach. After he passes, Katie says, "I said 'Hi' to him." Karen said, "That's nice, honey. What did he say to you?" "He said, Hi." Katie looks back at him. "Of course, I can *see his bottom!*" (*August, 1999*)

A Story, dictated by Katie:
"Once there was a little girl, her name was Katie G. And she played Barbie's a lot. She loved her Barbie's. But the little girl, named Katie found a Barbie wedding shoe. And she tried to put it on her Barbie that morning. She played with her brother with cars. She loved him a lot. So much she couldn't stop.

Once she said, "I love you." Once our friends came over and our friend is named… of course they were guests. Their name was Colleen and Daniel. Once my brother went to their house but I didn't. but me and mommy stayed home. While mommy was folding laundry I watched Little Mermaid. I love our friends. We played at our house. To make David feel Better. **The end. By Katie G."** (*October 15, 1999*)

THE TOOTH (dictated by Katie)

"Once I was walking on the beach with my friends, Kristin & Sarah, and my brother David. We were going to find some treasures. I was happy. And there we had a snack. I lost my tooth; it was very loose one, of course.

When we got back in the car, I said to Mommy, "Hey! I think I lost my tooth!" Mom said, "Really? Wow!" Then she took a look. Sure enough, I did lost my tooth. Then we had a little play date, and I showed my friend, Kristin, the place where I lost my tooth. She said, "Oooh."

My brother wanted to play airplane. Then he wrote the Tooth Fairy a note. I can't remember what the note said. **Oh, I just remembered!**

Dear Tooth Fairy,

My sister lost a tooth. Since we couldn't find it on the beach, I wrote this note to explain it (since my sister couldn't write so well).

Sincerely,

David Gerstenberger

Then my brother drew cartoons showing me losing the tooth on the beach and me in bed with the Tooth Fairy looking over me. I put my note under my pillow and the next morning, I saw a dollar under my pillow. **The End.**

<u>*A conversation with Mom about God*</u>

Karen: God is invisible

Katie: He is real!

Karen: Yes, but you cannot see Him. He is like the wind…. You can see what it does to things, you can feel it, but you can't see it. You can't smell God, either.

Katie: I smelled him

Karen: Really? What did he smell like?

Katie: Like raspberry. He had a raspberry bubble bath. *(August, 1999)*

Katie's Dreams

Katie's list of things she wanted to be, after she realized she was dying. This list comes from numerous conversations with her Mom.

- She wanted to travel to places like Paris, Rome, Japan – or "The World" in general
- Be a child author, a fashion designer, go to Jr. High, High School, college, and get a job
- Get married, be a mother, aunt and finally a grandmother
- Be a good sister – she accomplished that despite the illness
- Make enough money to live a nice, modest life with good things

"In the last 11 months, Katie grew up a great deal. She matured in grace, humor, strength and awareness during her treatment and recovery. Everyone who met her fell in love with her. She made wonderful connections with people everywhere.

"In conclusion: Gregg, Karen and David hope, in coming here to share in this celebration, that you will take away with you some knowing, some spark of Katie's qualities and of her life, and that you will keep her memory in a way that feels natural to you."

Celebrating Katie's Life, cont'd
August 22, 2007 **led** by Beverly Gaines

"Faith, Hope and love - and the greatest of these is love….

- Gregg & Karen and David spoke of the overwhelming support and prayers from everyone – known and unknown, in response to this tragedy.
- An international wave of love and support that has nurtured and sustained them over this last year.

"And in the following are Gregg, Karen and David's own words to you:

- *The outpouring of love has been beyond our dreams of what actually existed in the world. It is like an aquifer, it rose up….*
- *As if there was a "crack," an opening, in the heart of the world. Crisis occurs; love brings forth compassion, and love leads where it will, into the flames. Each one responding out of love, with who they are, bringing their own gifts to the situation, in their own style/way, as an offering of love.*
- *It's bigger than we are, than the situation, than anything you can imagine. One of the things we have learned from this is how huge love is and how present - even in the darkest place.*
- *And both things are true - there are dark places and love exists. You don't have to deny the darkness or pretend.*

- *What Katie did was face her journey with courage, feistiness, anger, humor, grief, and she found joy and laughter and love.*
- *We saw the strength growing within her, the qualities of who she truly was.*
- *The whole thing was held in love. We didn't get the outcome we wanted. "We didn't get what we asked for we got what we needed. Moment by moment."*
- *Important for all of us to name the tragedy: There is a Katie shaped hole in the world – over which, through which we will live – and through which the love of God has come blazing through.*
- *If you felt like you knew her, listen for her and let her inspire you – fearlessness, sassiness, humor – let this inspiration encourage you to give and love the world. It has been said that Christ has no hands on earth but ours (Teresa of Avila).*
- *Let Katie's life, struggle and death awaken you to the gifts of faith hope and love.*
- *We come from love, we journey in love, and we return to love.*

"Amen."

APPENDIX B:

Resources that have helped us

- Family
- Friends
- Hospital staff that knew and cared for Katie: Childlife, pastoral care, social work, nurses, doctors, physical therapists
- Prayer
- Quiet time at home, alone
- Going back to work and school (for Gregg & David)
- Spiritual community: spiritual director, friends from church, books by favorite writers, spiritual websites
- Massage therapy
- Exercise
- Travel – we took a trip a week after Katie's memorial

- Online Community: www.caringbridge.org, Team Unite, www.griefhaven.org, facebook, blogs (Compassionate Friends, Hospice publications…)
- Reading the works of others who are farther down the path
- Writing: my blog, Hopeful Parents, Blissfully Domestic, Redbook
- Sewing quilts and working for Katie's Comforters Guild
- Raising funds and awareness through the *Katie Gerstenberger Endowment for Cancer Research* at Seattle Children's Hospital
- Visiting Katie's park bench (on the waterfront in Poulsbo)
- Speaking/giving interviews to newspapers, *Connections* magazine, etc.
- Telling Katie's story to raise awareness and funds for a cure (and better treatment protocols)
- Encouraging other families on the journey
- Music
- Seattle Children's Hospital and Regional Medical Center: www.seattlechildrens.org
- Katie's Comforters Guild: www.katiescomfortersguild.blogspot.com
- The Katie Gerstenberger Endowment for Cancer Research: www.katiegerstenbergerendowment.blogspot.com
- Ronald McDonald House of Western Washington
- Hospice of Kitsap County

- Griefhaven: www.griefhaven.org. DVD, "Portraits of Hope" available for purchase on griefhaven's website; video clip, "Starting Over House" free on griefhaven's website
- www.caringbridge.org/visit/katiegerstenberger
- www.cancer.gov
- http://www.hopefulparents.org
- www.teamunite.net
- The Hutch School: www.hutchschool.org

Books:

- Armstrong, Lance, It's Not About the Bike
- Braestrup, Kate, Here if You Need Me
- Chodron, Pema, When Things Fall Apart
- D'Arcy, Paula, Gift of the Red Bird
- Haugk, Kenneth, Don't Sing Songs to a Heavy Heart
- Janes, Hodder and Keene, Childhood Cancer
- Keating, Thomas, The Kingdom of God is Like...
- Keene, Nancy, Chemo, Craziness and Comfort
- Kubler-Ross, Elisabeth, On Death and Dying
- Lozowski-Sullivan, Sheryl, Know Before You Go: The Childhood Cancer Journey
- Miller, James E., One You Love is Dying
- Miller, James E. with Susan C. Cutshall, The Art of Being a Healing Presence
- Nouwen, Henri, Bread for the Journey
- Rohr, Richard, Radical Grace, Everything Belongs, Things Hidden: Scripture as Spirituality

Blogs:

My blog: www.karengberger.blogspot.com
- http://desertyear.blogspot.com
- http://searchthesea.blogspot.com
- http://compelledtotruenorth.blogspot.com
- http://circlingmyhead.blogspot.com
- http://joemaui.blogspot.com
- http://crazysexylife.com
- http://inversion16.blogspot.com
- http://inspiredbyerin.blogspot.com
- http://notesfromthewall.blogspot.com
- http://nieniedialogues.blogspot.com
- http://www.glowinthewoods.com/home
- http://www.sheyerosemeyerphotography.com/blog (ex.: 3-2-2010)

Surviving the Death of a Child *(excerpt from a talk given by Karen Gerstenberger at the Seattle Children's Hospital Annual Memorial Service, June 2010)*

Who was Kathryn Emilie Gerstenberger? She was a bright light, and a joyful, sparkling presence. Katie was the younger of our two children. She was outgoing, funny, creative, sociable, spirited, strong-willed, courageous, a bit tempestuous and very feminine. She was the best friend of her brother, David, from the time she was born.

In school, Katie's favorite subjects were reading and recess. She loved movies and television. Her life's dreams were to be a model, an actress, a bridesmaid, an author, and to get married and have children. She was beautiful, inside and out. Healthy; the least likely person you could imagine getting seriously ill.

But Katie did get sick, in the autumn of 2006, and a battery of medical tests over several weeks failed to reveal why. When we came to Seattle Children's Hospital and heard the diagnosis of a huge, life-threatening tumor in her abdomen, it was "the end of the world, as we knew it," (the song by R.E.M. played over and over in my mind) and the beginning of a new life for our family.

We asked Katie what she wanted us to do to support her, and her response was, "I want us to be together as much as possible." So we moved into Ronald McDonald House. We became, to use an auto-racing term, Katie's "Pit Crew."

After 10 months of treatment, recovery and relapse, she passed away at home, in her own bed, with

Gregg, David and me beside her. We were shattered. We miss her every single day.

What is it like, now that she has passed on ahead of us?

We are learning to live, day by day, with her memory, and with our love for her as inspiration, instead of having her physical presence, with the delight, joy and comfort that was for us. We will never have what we had before, as a foursome, but we are grateful that we did have it. Some of our hopes and dreams will never come true, but other hopes and dreams will arise, and be realized – and some already have.

We get up each day, do our best with what is given, and adjust. Our family is now a different shape, with a "Katie-shaped hole" in it.

For a mental picture, think of a car with three wheels. Another image that I like is of metal that is put through a forging process: pressure changes the internal grain in the metal. The elements that make up the metal are the same, but they are re-formed under intense pressure. Metal is stronger after forging. Or, as Ernest Hemingway said, *"The world breaks everyone, and afterward, some are strong at the broken places."*

Our marriage has changed, because we have each changed. We are less exuberant, yet more patient. We know that we cannot always comfort each other, since we are all grieving, and differently. For example, I have a strong need to put my grief into words, but Gregg and David do not.

We honor Katie's memory in ways which are in keeping with her character, and which we believe would bring her happiness. For example:

- The Katie Gerstenberger Endowment for cancer research: donations have been made in her memory that would astonish her.
- Katie's Comforters Guild: hundreds of blankets like Katie's have been hand-made and donated in her memory to comfort patients at SCH.
- There are thousands of written words about Katie and our experiences on this journey, from blogs to newspaper, magazine and webzine articles.
- There is a bench in our waterfront park with Katie's name on it.
- There is education, "hope and empowerment," in talks that we've given since Katie started on this journey.
- Her photograph has been in front of hundreds of people – the girl who wanted to be an actress and model, is a model!
- Encouraging other families like ours, through groups like Team Unite and Griefhaven honors her memory.
- People give generously to causes that help those facing cancer, because Katie lived – and died– and her story inspires them to do what they can to make the world a better place.

The grief journey after Katie's passing has changed with the years: the first year included shock, rebellion, anger, tears, physical pain, hope (in God) and exhaustion; the second year: acceptance, deeper awareness of loss, gratitude for the good that we still have, and (more) efforts to keep bitterness from taking root; and now, the third year: looking outward, working to make a difference in the world, and listening for direction in our next phase of life as our son leaves home for college.

Whether your child lived a few hours or all the way to adulthood, whether his passing was sudden, or the result of a long illness, we share the experience of *the reversal of nature's pattern*: we have buried our young. Everything in us screams that this is WRONG. And it is.

But I want you to know, in the midst of your grief, that there is comfort and fellowship waiting for you. We can survive this. Our pain will change and it will become easier to live with. I have learned this from others who are farther down this road than we are, and I have seen it happening to us over the past nearly-three years. I want to share that HOPE with you.

During an important conversation with me, Katie made a motion as if she took a piece of her heart, put it in mine, and said, "Now, I'll always be in here." I did the same to her, and you know, it's true: she IS always in here, and she always will be. When I relax and listen, I know that she is with me.

How we have changed: I care deeply about my family's feelings, but I also know that I'm not responsible for them. We know that we cannot necessarily be the first line of comfort for each other, since we are **all** grieving, and grieving differently. For example, my husband went back to his job, and David to his school, but my job as a stay-at-home mother has changed dramatically. I have one child, a young man, to care for, and he is going to graduate and leave home soon. I do not get to finish caring for Katie as she grows up to leave home, because she is gone already. The realization that my career as a stay-at-home mother is ending prematurely - the enforced career change/retirement, is a big life-adjustment, for me.

At first, I felt a bit frantic about Katie's legacy. Since she was only 12 when she passed, it troubled me greatly that she didn't get to do what she had dreamed of doing, and that I wasn't able to protect her, rescue her, and give her a future; it wasn't in my power. So I felt impelled to carry her legacy, to lift a torch with her light on it, and tell people about her. I wrote a lot on my blog, to release emotions and avoid bitterness. I wanted to *tell the truth* about our experiences, so I did that.

As time went on, I began to see that Katie's life, and her legacy, are *hers*. I don't have to worry about it.

I used to go to the beach when I was stressed or sad, and walking there (and looking for beach glass) helped me. Now, it's harder to do this and feel comfort. I remember taking the children there and I feel the loss in a new way.

It is important to me not to allow my life to be a "negative" legacy for Katie. I have a deep desire to honor her memory in a way that bears witness to her character: joy, love, humor and spiciness.

I pray that your grief will ease, day by day, and that your child's precious life will continue to inspire you and fill your heart with love.

If I were to offer a piece of survival advice, it would be this: be gentle with yourself and your family. Be true to yourself. Your heart and your gut will give you what you need to know, one moment at a time.

For Medical Professionals

This book contains a number of "pop-out" quotes, which are the most important things for you to remember. Here they are again, in list form:

- I thought, "We've already answered these questions; when is someone going to answer **our** questions?"
- At first, it was overwhelming, meeting so many people across disciplines that were new to us; it took time to become accustomed to having our quiet, ordinary, private life invaded.
- Waiting on the gurney was a Beanie Baby, and seeing that relaxed her - and me. It was a sign that we were in a children's hospital - a place where they understand the heart of a child.

- I said, "I'm so glad to hear that. I was really starting to dislike you, because all you ever did was give us bad news!"
- No matter who we are in the "outside world," we are stripped down to our essence in the hospital… it is good to be mindful that the people you encounter are, to a large extent, more naked than they have ever been, and more frightened.
- We asked Katie, "What can we do to give you the most support? What would help you the most?" She answered, "I want us to be together as much as possible."
- I love the fact that Seattle Children's Hospital understands that we know our child better than anyone.
- I will always remember that moment, because Dr. Brogan didn't minimize my fear.
- Rightly or wrongly, appearances can create unexpected responses to the team.
- Human beings have "background programs" which are operating all of the time, and in such a stressful time, we can focus an intense dislike on someone that has nothing to do with him as a person.
- It was imperative to me to communicate to this doctor who & what kind of family she was dealing with; I needed to know that she had the same level of commitment that I had, & I needed to see it in her eyes.
- Katie's physical therapist won my heart by "thinking outside of the box"

- To watch your child suffer, when you want only to protect her...over a period of days, weeks and months, is hard work. Even the nicest, best-mannered, kindest person will show strain under such conditions.
- That was the night when it dawned on me that it could always be worse.
- We did not want to put Katie through the agony of treatment, if she was going to die no matter what we tried.
- It gave us pause to know that what we were doing to try to save our child's life could also possibly harm her, in the long run.
- It's a good idea to pause before entering our room, and take a moment to breathe, because we might be in the midst of a sacred or painful conversation.
- Once a week, Gregg & I would go out to dinner. People in our community were generous, donating gift cards or money to help us to be able to afford to do this. I believe it helped our marriage - and our sanity.
- Intense stress was so much a part of our daily life that I felt we were all just one degree away from craziness.
- I felt trapped, sometimes...this is not the life we were used to; it's not the life that we would like to give to our children, and it's not a path we have chosen.
- I love Seattle Children's Hospital, especially for the fact that we never had to send Katie

<u>alone</u> into an experience that was upsetting or frightening to her.

- They could not promise us that she would live through the surgery, which involved removing her left adrenal gland, left kidney, a lobe of her liver, and her inferior vena cava.
- It was helpful and comforting to see Katie go to her surgery with someone we knew, someone with whom she was at ease, and who she trusted.
- I will always love that surgeon for taking the time to bravely tell us this terrible news, face to face, with seriousness, composure and compassion.
- No one had prepared us for how different Katie would look after her surgery.
- Immediately following Katie's surgery, we were not encouraged to sleep in her room. I feel uncomfortable about that to this day. I felt guilty and uncomfortable *every night* when we left the CICU to go to sleep at Ronald McDonald House.
- I can't adequately describe how much the thought of her open wound (covered with a dressing, but not closed with sutures) troubled me.
- As a mother, the desire to help when your child is so badly hurt is very powerful – I would say it is unstoppable.
- It was important to me that my input was respected, because **I knew Katie**, and was thus able to advocate - to "mother" her - even while

she was unconscious in the ICU. It made me feel much less helpless, less restless, and more useful.

- These little moments add up; they help us to form a relationship that goes beyond doctor-patient-family member, to a real connection as human beings.

- It may sound strange, but I have happy memories of the CICU, because the staff helped me to endure the strains of Katie's illness, and to grow while doing so. I learned to advocate for her as an essential part of Katie's team. That made an enormous, positive impact on how I felt while enduring a very difficult time.

- Katie did not feel up to facing a crowd of "strange" people, first thing in the morning. Rounds began with questions such as, "Have you passed gas today?" Try to imagine a beautiful, 12-year old girl facing this question; she did not want to discuss that issue.

- One of the things I appreciate about family-centered care is the way the staff speaks to the patient – they never talked over Katie's head, but spoke directly to her.

- Our Hematology-Oncology Childlife worker, Julie, shared some "tricks of the trade" with Katie, in order to make the removal of her stitches and drains easier. She coached Katie through these new experiences. The value of this kind of care is crucial to feeling less overwhelmed and more empowered.

- Privacy is rare and precious in a hospital, and it is important for staff to respect it, particularly volunteers.
- I remember looking into the surgeon's eyes and thinking, *This must sound crazy to him*, but I was thinking about Katie's future. Most important, of course, was her survival, and after that, her fulfillment as a human being.
- Although we would have much preferred "no evidence of disease," we did not panic at the results of the PET scan.
- Katie asked me, "What if the cancer comes back? What if I die?" I answered her, "If it's humanly possible, we'll get you out of this; we will do everything in our power to save your life."
- Katie was spinning out of control, because she could not integrate what she had been through into her old life. It's hard to imagine being 12 years old, and not knowing whether you are going to live or die…her childhood had effectively ended.
- No one knows what it is like, unless they have walked this path, and even then, each family's dynamics and pre-existing conditions are different.
- This moment of utter family breakdown was one of the lowest points on our journey. The emotional chaos which Katie was displaying was one of the many side effects of her cancer diagnosis and treatment.
- It takes great amounts of love, patience and compassion for a marriage to survive the

extreme situations like those I have described here.

- Her doctor said, "Katie, I promised that I would never lie to you. I don't have good news for you today; your cancer is back."

- We learned that some parents will do anything to prolong their child's life, even when the end is clearly near, but we did not feel that way. We wanted to give Katie the best quality of life she could possibly have – and we did not want her to experience any more suffering.

- As I tried to be polite, my mind was screaming: I'm trying to go home – we live over an hour away – we were just told that our daughter is going to die - could I please just have the drugs NOW!

- Katie took to calling Amy "the quack," and said, "She's here to help me die!" to which I replied, "No, she is here to make your life easier."

- When Katie was dying, we experienced similar emotional issues to those at the beginning of her illness: shock, disbelief, sadness.

- She began to tell me how she felt about her own death, her life's dreams and her sadness over the things that she was going to miss. This was very hard to bear, but listening was something I could do to help ease her pain.

- Open-hearted listening was a precious gift that I could give to Katie. There was so little I could do to "make it better," but listening was something that could help ease her pain. So I listened, and I grieved with her.

- The thought of a child going on without her parents, her family, is a gut-wrenching one to a mother, whose every instinct from conception is to keep her child safe – to love, tend, comfort and provide for her child's needs. Everything in me screamed that Katie needed her family with her.
- Katie found that, just before the surges of pain occurred, she experienced an "aura" that predicted them. She had two severe episodes that caused her to cry out in pain, before she learned to identify this aura. At one point, she screamed, "I want to die NOW!" That is a searing, traumatic memory.
- Katie looked directly at me and said, *"You stay with me."* I had a strong sense that this was a private, individual transition and that I wasn't to interfere.
- We never asked her to "fight cancer;" we never asked her *not to die.*
- "We didn't get what we asked for; we got what we needed."
- Compassion, listening, respect are precious gifts to patients and their families.

For Friends and Family: What to Do/What Not to Do

Many concerned friends and family members wonder how they can help when there is a health crisis or a death. Here are some concrete ideas that you can practice to help those you care about who are in difficulty.

1. Offer **concrete help.*** Do not say, "Call if you need anything," because they won't.
2. Listen to whatever they need to say.
3. Ask if they want to go out for coffee, a walk or a meal. Offer a gift card to a favorite restaurant or store.
4. Ask if they feel like talking before you start a conversation.

5. Do not ask if you can hug them. If you have to ask, the answer is "No."
6. Do not drop in. Always email, call or text first.
7. Do not expect a "Thank You" note or a call. Sometimes it just cannot be done.
8. Do not say, "I know just how you feel." You don't.
9. Do not say, "God only takes the prettiest flowers, the best, etc." Even if this were true, it would not be comforting.
10. Do not say, "She is in a better place," "At least his suffering is over," or try to point out "the good" in the tragedy. Doing that will not bring comfort.
11. Do not compare illnesses or tragedies. This is not a contest.
12. Do not express pity. Compassion and solidarity are good; pity is demeaning.
13. Tragedy is not contagious.
14. Share your fond memories of the deceased. People like an opportunity to talk about their beloved ones, and to hear that you care and remember.
15. Do not be afraid to speak the name of the deceased.
16. Do not call cancer "The Big C" or speak of it as a "fight." Cancer is not a fight; it's an ambush, a terrorist attack.
17. Do not assume that the bereaved share your faith, or your views on life after death.
18. Ask how they are doing today, and really listen to the answer.

19. Ask if they want company.
20. Feeling strong emotions is acceptable, but be responsible for your own. Sharing is okay; "dumping" is not.

Remember: You cannot fix this; do not try. Just be present in caring and love. It is enough.

*Concrete examples of things that are helpful:

*Meals: offer to bring a meal on a certain day. Ask about food allergies or preferences. Keep it simple, nutritious, tasty and re-heatable.

*Gift Cards *Lawn or Garden Care *Pet Care
*Housecleaning *Babysitting/child care *Greeting
                                                  Cards

*Small gifts: a candle, a pretty teacup, a small bouquet, a coffee card

*Chores: addressing "thank you" notes, walking the dog, etc.

*Errands: pick up prescriptions, buy groceries, pick up dry cleaning, trips to the Post Office…

*Uplifting books, fun magazines, puzzles or crafts to keep patient and caregiver mentally active

Other ways to help:

Organize a blood drive or bone marrow drive
Hold a garage sale or bake sale to raise funds
*Write an article or give an interview to raise awareness
Make a blanket to comfort the patient or family members
Pray, meditate, light candles

"10 Grief Lessons for Others" found on www.caringbridge.org:

"1. <u>BE THERE FOR ME</u>. If you are my friend, reach out, talk to me, hold my hand, hug me. Know that even though we may say we are all right, we will never be all right again.

"2. <u>WE ARE DIFFERENT.</u> Understand that what has happened will change us forever and if you are my friend, you will accept me for what I have become, for who I am now, a person with different goals and different priorities. What was once important to me may no longer have any meaning.

"3. <u>BE A GOOD LISTENER.</u> We want above all else to talk about our loved one. To us, they will always be alive in our hearts, and we don't want others to forget them either. Don't be afraid to mention their names in our conversations. They were real people at one time, even though they are no longer with us. They had hopes and dreams we'd still like to share with others. Please don't pretend they never existed.

"4. <u>NO ONE ELSE KNOWS HOW I FEEL.</u> We all grieve differently. Please don't tell me you know how I feel. You don't. Rather than asking me, "How are you feeling?" ask me "What are you feeling?" I can probably give you a more honest answer.

"5. <u>I MAY GRIEVE FOR A VERY LONG TIME.</u> There is no set time limit to my grief. It may take me two years; it may take me five years. I have to do what is comfortable for me. Be patient. I will do the best I can in whatever amount of time it takes.

"6. <u>KEEP IN TOUCH.</u> Call me once in a while. I promise to do the same. Invite me to lunch or to a movie. I will eventually go, because I will eventually feel better. Don't give up on me and don't forget me. I am trying to do the best I can right now.

"7. <u>I MAY CRY AT TIMES IN FRONT OF YOU.</u> Please don't be embarrassed, and I won't be either. Besides being a natural emotion, crying is also a cleansing emotion. By crying I can relieve a lot of anger, frustration, guilt and stress. And best of all, I feel much better after a good cry.

"8. <u>I PUT A MASK ON FOR THE PUBLIC.</u> Don't assume just because I am functioning during the day that I am "over it." I will never get "over it." I try to function normally because I have no other choice. You should see me when the day is over, and I am in the privacy of my own home and free to let my emotions out. My day mask comes off and I am just a mother, aching for her child.

"9. <u>SOME DAYS MAY BE OVERWHELMING.</u> The slightest thing can trigger a bad time. It can be a song, a place I go, a holiday, a wedding or even smells or sounds. If I break down and start crying or seem to be in another world, it is because I am thinking of my loved one and longing for what I will never have again. I may need to try different things before I find what will be right for me in my new life. Encourage me to reach for the stars.

"10. <u>LET ME DO WHATEVER MAKES ME HAPPY.</u> We will never forget our loved one. The pain never leaves. It just softens a little with time. We eventually function again, feel hope again, find joy in our lives. It is a long road that we travel, but with the help of friends and relatives who understand a little of how we feel and what we are going through, perhaps that road will lead to new paths to enrich our lives in new ways understanding and empathy were deep, and they gave me assurance that he was going to survive this.

Ways to Help

*I*f you would like to contribute to or join Katie's Comforters Guild (part of Seattle Children's Hospital's Guild Association), or to start such a group in your own community, please visit www. katiescomfortersguild.blogspot.com (the history of Katie's Comforters is told in Chapter Eight of this book). If you join us, you can sew, crochet, knit or use fleece to make blankets for new patients at Seattle Children's Hospital. You can also raise funds, or donate funds, gift cards & materials. Any form of help that suits you is welcome! Our goal is to supply the entire hospital with homemade blankets for comfort, on an ongoing basis.

Katie used her quilt as a: *reminder of home *cloak, to hide under

*mask, to block smells that bothered her   *lap blanket, to warm her legs

*coat, to keep warm   *blinder, to avoid unpleasant sights

*bathrobe, over her pajamas   *distraction, studying it instead of watching procedures

Here is an easy pattern for sewing a simple quilt, like Katie's. To make one blanket, you will need:

★ 1 yard **Cotton Flannel**
★ 1 yard **Cotton Quilt Fabric, color-coordinated with the flannel**
★ 1 – 2 pkgs. **Wright's Satin Blanket Binding, 4.75 yds. (4.35 m), 100% polyester, color-coordinated with the fabrics**
★ 1 yard of ¾ to 1" **thick Batting (not cotton)**
★ **Thread to match**

* **Wash & dry** both pieces of fabric. If one piece is larger than the other, lay that piece, right-side down, on your work surface. Smooth it out from the center to the edges; place the batting on top of it. Lay the other piece of fabric on top of the batting, right side up; smooth out the wrinkles.

*Pin all 3 layers together in at least 5 places in the middle & around the quilt. Trim the edges so that the 3 pieces are all the same size.

*Unwrap the satin binding. Starting at one corner of the quilt, **pin** the binding around each side, with the points of the pins facing the outside edge of the blanket. When you come to a corner, fold the binding to make the turn (a mitred corner). You are sandwiching the 2 layers of fabric & the batting between the 2 layers of the satin binding. Pin all four sides of the quilt with blanket binding, turning the end of the binding under & overlapping the beginning with the end piece.

*Using a **strong** zigzag stitch, **sew** along the edges of the binding, all of the way around the blanket. Check the underside of the binding to be sure that you are capturing it as you are sewing the top. When you get to the end of the blanket binding, you may fold the binding under & stitch it closed, or finish it as you like, to make a clean seam.

*In the center of the quilt, **stitch** by machine (or by hand) where your pins are tacking the three layers in place. Do this at least 5 times (quilting) to keep the batting from shifting with wear (& love & washing). *Please **TRIPLE-CHECK** your quilt and **REMOVE ALL PINS** before donating it to the Volunteer Office at Seattle Children's Hospital – this is vital for patients' safety!* Thank you!

More Ways to Help

Seattle Children's Hospital's Guild Association offers much information and many resources for people who wish to support the hospital and its work in a variety of ways. Please visit: http://www.seattlechildrens.org/ways-to-help/guilds.

For information about the **Katie Gerstenberger Endowment for Cancer Research** at Seattle Children's Hospital, please visit: www.katiegerstenbergerendowment.blogspot.com. In accordance with Katie's own request, her endowment supports solid tumor research at Seattle Children's Hospital's Center for Childhood Cancer Research. The principal remains invested, and the income is drawn off to use in research to find cures for solid tumors. For information on how to make a donation to Katie's endowment, please visit http://www.seattlechildrens.org/ways-tohelp/donate/.

The Ben Towne Pediatric Cancer Research Foundation is a 501(c)(3) non-profit public charity supporting the most current research to find cures for all pediatric cancers. Please visit www.bentownefoundation.org to learn more about the wonderful work they are doing, and how you can help.

About the Author

Karen Boren Gerstenberger is a writer, wife and mother who lives with her family (including cats Latte & Liger) on the shores of Puget Sound, Washington. She enjoys reading, fitness walking, travel, good food and anything involving the beach. Karen founded Katie's Comforters Guild at Seattle Children's Hospital in order to provide handmade blankets to all patients of the hospital, and she works to raise awareness about, and funds for, pediatric cancer research. You are welcome to visit her blog: www.karengberger.blogspot.com.

Made in the USA
Charleston, SC
12 February 2012